cookies

cookies

Bethany Heald
photography by Jean Cazals

getting started

Getting Started

Cookies, of course, are delicious in their own right, but they can be made that little bit extra special by decorating them. You don't need to spend an age on this – many cookies can be decorated in a couple of minutes by simply sprinkling on some nuts or seeds. Cookie decorating is also a great way of getting your children involved, because they will be even more enthusiastic about helping with weighing, mixing, and shaping if they know they will have all the fun of decorating the cookies as well. You could even have a cookie decorating party for a child's birthday. Just present them with a selection of different shapes and sizes of cookies and various different icings, plus cutters, edible icing pens, glitters and sprinkles and let them create. If you are worried about them creating a mess in the process, a good idea is to lay down a large sheet of plastic or newspaper under the table to catch any spills. Older children can also make their own cookies using the stencils on pages 88–93, or even design their own stencils.

There are various types of cookie doughs in this book: some are soft and spoonable, some are rolled into balls in your hands and flattened, some need to be rolled out like pastry.

Equipment List:

- baking sheets
- various shapes and sizes of cookie cutters
- wire racks
- spatula
- metal palette knife or fish slice
- different sizes of mixing bowls
- electric hand whisk (optional)
- food processor
- rolling pin
- **piping nozzles:** fine writing, star shape
- **piping bags:** either disposable, plastic or washable fabric. (For a DIY option, cut a large triangle of baking parchment, then cross two of the points over to make a cone shape until they meet at the other side with a tiny hole at the point. Secure the bag by folding over the tails of paper.)
- fine sieves for dusting
- paintbrushes for fine decorating
- nonstick baking parchment
- nonstick silicon mats (reusable)
- **stencil-making equipment:** greaseproof or tracing paper, pencil, scissors, small knife or scalpel

Various types of food dyes are available including liquid, paste and natural dyes.
You can buy small tubes of writing icing in different colours from larger supermarkets; they usually come in a pack of four different colours.

Regal icing is quick and simple to make and is very useful for decorating cookies because it can be rolled out and cut using the same cutter that you used for the cookie dough. You can add colouring to the icing and knead it in to give an even colour, but remember that the paste dye is much more concentrated than the liquid so you should alter the amount used accordingly.

Regal Icing

1 tablespoon liquid glucose
1 egg white
500 g/1 lb/4¼ cups icing (confectioners') sugar, sifted

Place the glucose and egg white in a large bowl and stir together just to break up the egg white. Gradually add the icing sugar and stir until you can't stir in any more, then tip out on to a cool surface and knead in the remaining sugar. Continue to knead until you have a smooth ball without any lumps. Wrap the ball tightly in clingfilm and then in a plastic bag until ready to use.

Storage:
All the sweet cookies can be stored in an airtight container for one week. The savoury cookies are best eaten within three or four days when stored in airtight containers such as plastic Tupperware boxes, tins, or glass or ceramic cookie jars. If freezing the cookies, it is best to do so before cooking them – shape the cookie dough into the desired shapes on nonstick baking parchment and stack up in a freezerproof container. They can be frozen for up to three months. When ready to bake the cookies, just take out the number you wish to make and bake from frozen, increasing the baking time by 2–3 minutes.

with coffee

Honey and Ginger Cookies

Preparation time: 25 minutes
Resting time: 1 hour
Cooking time: 10–12 minutes
Makes 24

250 g/9 oz/2¼ cups unsalted butter, softened
350 g/12 oz/1½ cups soft brown sugar
4 tablespoons honey
3 tablespoons chopped stem ginger
2 tablespoons syrup from stem ginger jar
1 tablespoon grated fresh ginger (optional)
1 tablespoon ground ginger
285 g/10 oz/2 cups plain (all-purpose flour)
2 teaspoons baking powder
½ teaspoon fine salt
75 g/3 oz/1 cup rolled oats

Cream the butter, sugar and honey together until pale and creamy. Add the stem ginger, stem ginger syrup and fresh ginger (if using) and stir. Sift the ground ginger, flour, baking powder and salt together and fold into the mixture with the oats using a large metal spoon. Bring the mixture together by kneading for 30 seconds. Roll it into a log shape 5 x 5 x 30 cm/2 x 2 x 12 in, wrap in clingfilm and refrigerate for at least 1 hour. At this stage you can freeze the dough if desired for 2–3 months; when you want to use it, thaw the dough slightly then cut into slices and extend the cooking time by 2 minutes.

Preheat the oven to 180°C/350°F/gas mark 4. Grease and line 2 baking sheets with nonstick baking parchment.

Remove the dough log from the fridge, slice into 5 mm/¼ in discs, place on the baking sheets and bake for 10–12 minutes until golden on top. Leave to cool on the baking sheets for 2 minutes before transferring to wire racks to cool completely. The rolled oats in the dough are the decoration in this recipe because when they cook they turn a lovely golden colour.

Rosewater and Pistachio Cookies

Preparation time: 25 minutes
Cooking time: 8–10 minutes
Makes 24

100 g/3½ oz/scant ½ cup unsalted butter, softened
200 g/7 oz/1 cup golden granulated sugar
2 medium eggs, at room temperature
3 tablespoons rosewater
285 g/10 oz/2 cups plain (all-purpose) flour
1 teaspoon baking powder
½ teaspoon fine salt
110 g/4 oz/1 cup pistachio nuts, roughly chopped

To decorate
2 roses, free of pesticides, of whatever colour you wish
1 egg white
60 g/2 oz/¼ cup white sugar

Preheat the oven to 190°C/375°F/gas mark 5. Grease and line 2 baking sheets with nonstick baking parchment.

Cream the butter and sugar together until pale and fluffy using a wooden spoon or electric hand whisk. Beat in the eggs one at a time, followed by the rosewater. Sift the flour, baking powder and salt together and stir into the mixture. Add the pistachio nuts and stir to incorporate. Drop heaped tablespoons on to the baking sheets, leaving a 5 cm/2 in space between each one, as they will spread when baking, and flatten with dampened fingers into 5 mm/¼ in thick discs. Bake for 8–10 minutes or until the cookies start to turn golden. Leave to cool on the baking sheets for 2 minutes before transferring to a wire rack to cool completely.

While the cookies are cooling, you can prepare the frosted rose petals. Carefully separate the petals and spread out on a wire rack. Whisk the egg white lightly just to loosen it without it going fluffy, then paint the egg white on to both sides of the petals using a paint brush or pastry brush. Allow any excess egg white to drip off before sprinkling with the sugar. Place one rose petal on each cooled cookie before eating.

Orange Blossom and Almond Cookies

Preparation time: 25 minutes
Cooking time: 10 minutes
Makes 24

100 g/3½ oz/⅔ cup blanched almonds
100 g/3½ oz/½ cup unsalted butter, softened
100 g/3½ oz/½ cup golden granulated sugar
1 medium egg, at room temperature
2 tablespoons orange blossom water
225 g/8 oz/1¾ cups plain (all-purpose) flour
1 teaspoon baking powder
½ teaspoon fine salt

To decorate
250 g/9 oz/2 cups icing (confectioners') sugar, sifted
2 tablespoons fat free vanilla yogurt
1 tablespoon orange or lime juice
1 teaspoon finely grated zest of 1 orange or lime

Preheat the oven to 180°C/350°F/gas mark 4. Grease and line 2 baking sheets with nonstick baking parchment.

Roast the almonds on a baking sheet for 10–15 minutes, turning them over halfway so that they colour evenly. Remove from the oven when golden brown and tip on to a plate. Cream the butter and sugar together until pale and fluffy using a wooden spoon or electric hand whisk. Beat in the egg and orange blossom water until fully incorporated. Sift the flour, baking powder and salt together. Once the almonds have cooled, roughly chop them and add to the mixture with the dry ingredients. Fold in until you have a light dough. Roll the dough into golfball-sized balls, place on the baking sheets and flatten with dampened fingers. Bake for 10–12 minutes until golden brown. Leave to cool on the baking sheets for 2 minutes before transferring to a wire rack.

While the cookies are cooling, mix the icing sugar, yogurt, orange or lime juice and zest in a bowl until smooth. When the cookies are completely cool, dip half of each cookie into the icing mixture and return to the wire rack to set.

Saffron, Honey and Pine Nut Cookies

Preparation time: 25 minutes
Cooking time: 10 minutes
Makes 24

¼ teaspoon saffron threads
1 tablespoon water
100 g/3½ oz/½ cup unsalted butter, softened
100 g/3½ oz/½ cup soft dark brown sugar
4 tablespoons runny honey
1 medium egg, at room temperature
1 teaspoon vanilla extract
225 g/8 oz/1¾ cups plain (all-purpose) flour
1 teaspoon baking powder
½ teaspoon fine salt

To decorate
110 g/4 oz/1 cup pine nuts

Preheat the oven to 180°C/350°F/gas mark 4. Grease and line 2 baking sheets with nonstick baking parchment.

Soak the saffron threads in the water and set aside.

Meanwhile, cream the butter, sugar and honey together until fluffy and slightly lighter in colour (10 minutes with a wooden spoon, 2–3 minutes with an electric hand whisk!). Add the egg and beat into the mixture. Stir in the saffron and water mixture and vanilla extract. Sift the flour, baking powder and salt together and stir into the mixture until all the dry ingredients have been incorporated. Sprinkle the pine nuts on to a flat plate. Roll the dough into golfball-sized balls, flatten with dampened fingers into 5 mm/¼ in thick discs, then press them into the pine nuts before placing on the baking sheets with the pine nut side uppermost. Bake for 10 minutes or until the pine nuts are golden in colour. Leave to cool on the baking sheets for 1–2 minutes before transferring to a wire rack to cool completely.

Korean Cookies

Preparation time: 15–20 minutes
Cooking time: 9 minutes
Makes 30–35

Syrup
4 tablespoons stem ginger syrup (from jar)
50 g/2 oz/¼ cup granulated sugar
75 g/3 oz/¼ cup honey
125 ml/4 fl oz/½ cup water

250 g/8 oz/2 cups plain (all-purpose) flour
pinch of fine salt
3 tablespoons sesame oil
3 tablespoons runny honey
2 tablespoons rice vinegar
2 tablespoons orange juice
2 tablespoons water
125 ml/4 fl oz/½ cup vegetable oil

To decorate
30 g/1 oz/¼ cup pine nuts, roughly chopped
2 tablespoons ground cinnamon

These unusual fried cookies are made from a dough similar to a pastry dough. They are totally immersed in syrup, which makes them an extra special sticky treat best served warm. They will not have a chance to cool down as they will be eaten in a flash

Firstly, make the syrup. Place the stem ginger syrup, sugar, honey and water in a small pan, bring to the boil and simmer for 1–2 minutes, stirring constantly. Set aside.

Sift the flour into a bowl with the salt and pour in the sesame oil. Rub the mixture with your fingertips (as when making pastry) until it resembles fine breadcrumbs. Make a well in the centre of the flour. Mix the honey, rice vinegar, orange juice and water together in a small jug and pour into the well, stirring the liquid into the flour until you have a dry dough. Don't be tempted to add more water – the mixture will come together. Roll out the dough on a lightly floured surface until 5 mm/¼ in thick. Using a small heart-shaped cookie cutter, 4 x 4 cm/1½ x 1½ in, or the stencil on page 88, cut the dough into heart shapes. Heat the vegetable oil in a large frying pan over a low/medium heat. Add one-third of the hearts and fry for 1½ minutes on each side or until golden brown. If the oil is too hot, the outside of the cookies will brown before the dough is cooked inside. Remove with a slotted spoon and drain on kitchen paper. Repeat with the next 2 batches. Using tongs, dip the cookies into the warm syrup and place on a serving plate.

Place the pine nuts in a frying pan and fry over a medium heat for 2 minutes until golden brown on both sides. Sprinkle over the cinnamon and toasted pine nuts.

Lemon and Lime

Preparation time: 10 minutes
Cooking time: 8–10 minutes
Makes 20

100 g/3½ oz/½ cup unsalted butter, softened
200 g/7 oz/1 cup golden granulated sugar
1 medium egg, at room temperature
325 g/11½ oz/1 cup lemon curd
finely grated zest of 2 limes
285 g/10 oz/2 cups plain (all-purpose) flour
1 teaspoon baking powder
½ teaspoon fine salt

To decorate
1 egg white
grated zest of 2 limes or 1 lemon
1 tablespoon sugar

Preheat oven to 190°C/375°F/gas mark 5. Grease 2 baking sheets and line with nonstick baking parchment.

Place the butter and sugar in large bowl, beat until pale and fluffy using a wooden spoon or electric hand whisk. Add the egg and beat well to combine, stir in the lemon curd and lime zest. Sift together the flour, baking powder and salt and stir into the mixture.

Spoon heaped tablespoons of the mixture on to the prepared baking sheets leaving a 5 cm/2 in space between each one, as they will spread when baking. Flatten with dampened fingers into 2.5 mm/⅛ in thick discs. Bake the cookies in the oven for 8–10 minutes or until they start to turn slightly golden, remove from the oven and allow to cool on the baking sheets for 2–3 minutes before transferring to a wire rack to cool completely.

While the cookies are cooling prepare the decoration. Lightly beat the egg white and add the zest, then drain to remove the excess egg. Remove the zest and place it in a single layer on a plate, then sprinkle with sugar, tossing with a fork to evenly coat all of the zest with sugar. Scatter the zest over the cookies and serve immediately.

Marmalade and Ginger Cookies

Preparation time: 10 minutes
Cooking time: 10–15 minutes
Makes 24

100 g/3½ oz/½ cup unsalted butter, softened
200 g/7 oz/1 cup golden granulated sugar
2 medium eggs, at room temperature
300 g/10 oz/1 cup fine cut marmalade
90 g/3 oz/½ cup roughly chopped stem ginger
300 g/10 oz/2 cups plain (all-purpose) flour
1 teaspoon baking powder
2 tablespoons finely chopped stem ginger

I like to use Seville marmalade for these cookies but any good-quality marmalade will do fine. They are deliciously chewy and sticky on the inside with a crunchy edge.

Preheat the oven to 190°C/375°F/gas mark 5. Grease and line 2 or 3 baking sheets with nonstick baking parchment.

Place the butter and sugar in a food processor and blend on high for 2 minutes until slightly pale (you may need to stop and scrape down the sides every so often). Add one of the eggs and blend, then add the second egg and blend for a few seconds. Add the marmalade and stem ginger and pulse 5 or 6 times to combine. Sift the flour and baking powder together and tip into the food processor carefully, as you don't want to be covered in a cloud of flour! Replace the lid and pulse until the dough is well mixed. Drop heaped tablespoons on to the baking sheets, leaving a 5 cm/2 in space between each one, as they will spread when baking, and making sure that each is of a similar size so that they bake evenly. Flatten them slightly to about the thickness of your little finger, then sprinkle with the finely chopped ginger. Bake for 10–12 minutes; the baking sheet in the lower part of the oven may need to be moved up to the top when the cookies on the top are cooked. Leave to cool on the baking sheets for 2 minutes before transferring to wire racks to cool completely.

Shortbread Cookies

Preparation time: 15 minutes
Cooking time: 40–50 minutes
Makes 16

110 g/4 oz/½ cup golden caster sugar (superfine) sugar
240 g/8 oz/2 cups plain (all-purpose) flour
25 g/1 oz/¼ cup rice flour
175 g/6 oz/¾ cup butter
pinch of fine salt
finely grated zest of 1 lemon or orange

Shortbread is a cookie originally from Scotland.
The custom is to serve it at Christmas and New Year
but I find you can enjoy it at any time of the year.
This recipe is not the most common one but a less
heavy version.

Preheat the oven to 150°C/300°F/gas mark 2. Grease
2 x sandwich tins 15 cm/6 in in diameter with butter or
vegetable oil.

   Remove 2 tablespoons of the sugar and set aside to use
later to decorate. Sieve the remaining sugar and the flours
into a bowl. Cut the butter into small cubes and rub into the
flour and sugar using your fingertips until the mixture
resembles fine breadcrumbs. Add the lemon or orange zest
and gather together with your hands, kneading until you
have a soft dough. Be patient and don't be tempted to add
water – the mixture will eventually come together. Transfer
the dough evenly between the 2 sandwich tins and press
down to flatten. Score the dough in each sandwich tin into
8 triangular wedges with a sharp knife, then prick the surface
evenly with a fork to make whatever pattern you wish. Bake
for 40–50 minutes until golden on top. Remove from the
oven and sprinkle with the reserved sugar. Leave to cool in
the tins for 15 minutes before transferring to wire racks to
cool completely. When completely cool, carefully break up
the shortbread into wedges along the cut lines.

Pear and Cinnamon Cookies

Preparation time: 25 minutes
Cooking time: 10 minutes
Makes 24

700 g/1½ lb/3 large pears
4 small or 2 large cinnamon sticks
1 tablespoon caster (superfine) sugar
100 g/3½ oz/½ cup unsalted butter, softened
100 g/3½ oz/½ cup soft dark brown sugar
2 medium eggs, at room temperature
285 g/10 oz/2 cups plain (all-purpose) flour
1 teaspoon baking powder
½ teaspoon fine salt
1 teaspoon ground cinnamon

To decorate
2 tablespoons caster (superfine) sugar
1 teaspoon ground cinnamon

Preheat the oven to 180°C/350°F/gas mark 4. Grease and
line 2 baking sheets with nonstick baking parchment.

   Peel, core and chop the pears into equal-sized chunks of
about 1 cm/½ in and tip into a small pan with the cinnamon
sticks, sugar, and a teaspoon of water. Cook over a low
heat for 10 minutes or until the pears are soft. Remove the
cinnamon sticks and strain away the liquid, leaving just
the softened pear. Set aside to cool.

   Cream the butter and sugar together until light and fluffy,
then add the eggs one at a time. Stir in the cooled pears, then
sift the flour, baking powder, salt and cinnamon together and
fold in. Using a dessertspoon, drop golfball-sized dollops on
to the baking sheets, leaving a 5 cm/2 in space between each
one, as they will spread when baking, and flatten with
dampened fingers into 5 mm/¼ in thick discs. Bake for
10–12 minutes, or until golden brown. Leave to cool on the
baking sheets for 2 minutes.

   Mix the sugar and cinnamon together to make the
cinnamon sugar and sprinkle over the cookies before
transferring to a wire rack to cool completely.

Rum and Raisin Cookies

Preparation time: 25 minutes
Cooking time: 10 minutes
Makes 24

225 g/8 oz/1½ cups raisins
8 tablespoons/3 fl oz/⅓ cup dark rum
100 g/3½ oz/½ cup unsalted butter, softened
200 g/7 oz/1 cup dark brown sugar
1 medium egg, at room temperature
a few drops of vanilla essence
285 g/10 oz/2 cups plain (all-purpose) flour
1 teaspoon baking powder
½ teaspoon fine salt

As you bite into these cookies the raisins burst in your mouth and you get a hit of rum that is a delightful surprise to the unsuspecting. Definitely one for adults only.

Preheat the oven to 180°C/350°F/gas mark 4. Grease and line 2 baking sheets with nonstick baking parchment.

Place the raisins and rum in a small pan, bring to the boil and then reduce to a simmer for 15 minutes, until the raisins are plump and have absorbed most of the liquid. Set aside and leave to cool completely.

Cream the butter and sugar together until light and fluffy. Add the egg and beat into the mixture, then stir in the rummy raisins and vanilla essence. Sift the flour, baking powder and salt together and fold into the mixture gently until it forms a firm dough. Roll the dough into golfball-sized balls, place on the baking sheets and flatten with dampened fingers into 5 mm/¼ in thick discs. Bake for 10 minutes or until the cookies start to turn golden on top. Leave to cool on the baking sheets for 1–2 minutes before transferring to a wire rack to cool completely.

Banana and White Chocolate Cookies

Preparation time: 25 minutes
Cooking time: 10 minutes
Makes 20

120 g/4 oz/1 cup unsalted butter, softened
150 g/5 oz/¾ cup golden granulated sugar
50 g/2 oz/¼ cup soft brown sugar
1 medium egg, at room temperature
4 medium ripe bananas, peeled and mashed
a few drops of vanilla essence
175 g/6 oz/1¼ cups plain (all-purpose) flour
1 teaspoon baking powder
½ teaspoon fine salt
100 g/3½ oz/1 cup white chocolate, roughly chopped

To decorate
20 dried banana chips

These cookies are all the better if you use perfectly ripe bananas. The white chocolate adds a certain decadence and I find them irresistible served with a strong black coffee to cut through the richness.

Preheat the oven to 180°C/350°F/gas mark 4. Grease and line 2 baking sheets with nonstick baking parchment.

Cream the butter and sugars together until light and fluffy using a wooden spoon or electric hand whisk. Add the egg and beat into the mixture before adding the bananas and vanilla essence. Beat again until smooth. Sift the flour, baking powder and salt together and gently fold into the mixture with the white chocolate. Roll the dough into golfball-sized balls and flatten in your hands into 5 mm/¼ in thick discs. Place on the baking sheets and bake for 10 minutes or until the cookies start to turn golden on top.

To decorate, place a banana chip on each cookie as soon as they come out of the oven. Transfer to a wire rack to cool completely if you can wait that long – otherwise they are great served warm.

Bitter Chocolate with Gold Leaf

Preparation time: 25 minutes
Cooking time: 10 minutes
Makes 24

200 g/7 oz/2 cups dark chocolate (minimum 70% cocoa
   solids), broken into squares
100 g/3½ oz/½ cup unsalted butter, softened
100 g/3½ oz/½ cup soft dark brown sugar
2 medium eggs, at room temperature
1 teaspoon vanilla extract
285 g/10 oz/2 cups plain (all-purpose) flour
1 teaspoon baking powder
½ teaspoon fine salt
1 tablespoon cocoa powder

To decorate
200 g/7 oz/1 cup dark chocolate, melted
2 sheets of gold leaf

These cookies are the ultimate in decadence – not
only is there melted chocolate in the dough, but
the entire cookie is coated in yet more chocolate.
Needless to say it is vital that you use a good-quality
chocolate as so much of the flavour depends on it. You
may think I have taken leave of my senses by putting
a piece of gold leaf on a cookie, but trust me on this
one – it is edible and has been used for decorating
food since the Middle Ages. Gold leaf is available from
art shops as well as some specialist cake shops, but
do make sure that you get the real thing as some fake
gold leaf is not edible. If you are out to impress, this is
the cookie for you!

Preheat the oven to 180°C/350°F/gas mark 4. Grease and
line 2 baking sheets with nonstick baking parchment.

Melt the chocolate in a heatproof glass bowl over a pan of
simmering water, making sure that the bowl does not touch
the water as it could burn the chocolate. Once melted,
remove from the heat and set aside to cool slightly.

Cream the butter and sugar together until fluffy and
lighter in colour using a wooden spoon or electric hand
whisk. Beat in the eggs one at a time and, when fully
incorporated, stir in the melted chocolate. Sift the flour,
baking powder, salt and cocoa powder together and fold into
the mixture until a soft and sticky dough is formed. Using a
dessertspoon, drop golfball-sized dollops on to the baking
sheets and flatten with dampened fingers into 5 mm/¼ in
thick discs. Bake for 10–12 minutes.

Meanwhile, melt the chocolate for decorating (using the
same method as above) and set aside in a warm place.

Remove the cookies from the oven and leave to cool for
1 minute on the baking sheet before transferring to a wire
rack. Once completely cooled and hardened, drop each
cookie into the warm melted chocolate. Cover the entire
cookie in chocolate, then remove with a spoon and place on
a sheet of greaseproof paper. Before the chocolate sets
completely, break off small pieces of gold leaf and place one
in the centre of each cookie. I find this easiest using clean
tweezers, because if the gold leaf touches your hands it will
stick and you will have gold-plated hands! Leave to set – if
you can wait that long – then serve.

Chocolate and Pistachio Cookies

Preparation time: 25 minutes
Cooking time: 10 minutes
Makes 24

200 g/7 oz/2 cups milk (semi-sweet) chocolate, broken
    into squares
100 g/3½ oz/½ cup butter, softened
100 g/3½ oz/½ cup granulated sugar
100 g/3½ oz/½ cup dark soft brown sugar
1 medium egg, at room temperature
1 teaspoon vanilla essence
285 g/10 oz/2 cups plain (all-purpose) flour
1 teaspoon baking powder
½ teaspoon fine salt
110 g/4 oz/1 cup pistachio nuts, roughly chopped

To decorate
50 g/2 oz/¼ cup milk (semi-sweet) chocolate, melted
25 g/1 oz/¼ cup pistachio nuts, toasted

Preheat the oven to 190°C/375°F/gas mark 5. Grease and
line 2 baking sheets with nonstick baking parchment.

Melt the chocolate in a heatproof glass bowl over a pan of
simmering water, making sure that the bowl does not touch
the water as it could burn the chocolate. Leave simmering
until the chocolate has just melted and set aside to cool.

Meanwhile, cream the butter and sugars together until
pale and fluffy. Beat in the egg and vanilla essence and, once
incorporated into the mixture, stir in the melted chocolate.
Sift the flour, baking powder and salt together and fold into
the mixture with the pistachio nuts to form a wet dough.
Using a dessertspoon, drop spoonfuls on to the baking sheets
and flatten with dampened fingers into 5 mm/¼ in thick
discs. Bake for 10 minutes, or until just starting to change
colour. Leave to cool on the baking sheets for 1 minute
before transferring to a wire rack. Once cooled, place a
teaspoon of melted chocolate and a toasted pistachio nut in
the centre of each cookie. Leave to set then serve.

Coffee and Hazelnut Cookies

Preparation time: 25 minutes
Cooking time: 10–12 minutes
Makes 24

1 tablespoon milk
4 tablespoons coffee granules (or 4 tablespoons espresso coffee)
100 g/3½ oz/½ cup unsalted butter, softened
100 g/3½ oz/½ cup golden granulated sugar
100 g/3½ oz/½ cup soft dark brown sugar
1 medium egg, at room temperature
a few drops of vanilla essence
200 g/7 oz/1¾ cups plain (all-purpose) flour
1 teaspoon baking powder
½ teaspoon fine salt
100 g/3 oz/¾ cup roughly chopped hazelnuts

To decorate
50 g/2 oz/¼ cup dark chocolate (minimum 70% cocoa solids)
24 roasted coffee beans

Preheat the oven to 180°C/350°F/gas mark 4. Grease and
line 2 baking sheets with nonstick baking parchment.

Heat the milk in a microwave (or small pan) and add the
coffee granules. Alternatively, add the espresso coffee to the
cold milk. Set aside.

Cream the butter and sugars together until light and fluffy
using a wooden spoon or electric hand whisk. Beat in the egg
and vanilla essence, then stir in the milk mixture. Sift the flour,
baking powder and salt together and fold into the wet mixture
with the hazelnuts. Using a dessertspoon, drop golfball-sized
dollops on to the baking sheets and flatten with dampened
fingers. Bake for 10–12 minutes until golden brown.

Meanwhile, melt the chocolate in a heatproof glass bowl
over pan of simmering water, making sure that the bowl
does not touch the water. Then dip the coffee beans into the
melted chocolate and toss until all the beans are evenly coated.
Place a chocolate bean on each cookie as soon as you remove
them from the oven. Leave to cool on the baking sheets.

White Chocolate and Macadamia Nut Cookies

Preparation time: 20 minutes
Cooking time: 15 minutes
Makes 24

100 g/3½ oz/½ cup unsalted butter, softened
200 g/7 oz/1 cup golden granulated sugar
2 medium eggs, at room temperature
1 teaspoon vanilla extract
285 g/10 oz/2 cups plain (all-purpose) flour
1 teaspoon baking powder
½ teaspoon fine salt
200 g/7 oz/2 cups good-quality white chocolate, chopped
100 g/3½ oz/½ cup macadamia nuts, chopped

To decorate
50 g/2 oz/¼ cup white chocolate, broken into pieces

Preheat the oven to 190°C/375°F/gas mark 5. Grease and line 2 baking sheets with nonstick baking parchment.

Beat the butter and sugar together in a large bowl until pale and fluffy. Add one egg and the vanilla, beat well to combine before adding the second egg, beat again. Don't worry if the mixture curdles slightly, just take 1 tablespoon of the flour and beat into the mixture.

Sift together the flour, baking powder and salt and stir into the mixture. Then stir in the chocolate and macadamia nuts.

Roll the mixture into table tennis-sized balls and place on the baking sheets 5–8 cm/2–3 in apart. With dampened hands flatten the balls into discs about 5 mm/¼ in thick. Bake for 8–10 minutes or until the cookies turn pale gold around the edges. Allow to cool slightly, then transfer to a wire rack.

To decorate, place the chocolate in a heatproof glass bowl over a pan of gently simmering water, making sure that the bowl does not touch the water. Heat for 2–3 minutes or until completely melted. Take care not to overheat as this will cause the chocolate to split. Remove from the heat and cool slightly.

Dip a fork into the melted chocolate and quickly drizzle over the cooled cookies. It will take only a few minutes to set.

Chilli Chocolate Cookies

Preparation time: 20 minutes
Cooking time: 15 minutes
Makes 20

100 g/3½ oz/½ cup unsalted butter, softened
200 g/7 oz/1 cup soft dark brown sugar
2 medium eggs, at room temperature
285 g/10 oz/2 cups plain (all-purpose) flour
1 teaspoon baking powder
½ teaspoon fine salt
½ teaspoon hot chilli powder
200 g/7 oz/2 cups dark chocolate, chopped

To decorate
50 g/2 oz/¼ cup dark chocolate, roughly chopped
1 teaspoon chilli flakes

Preheat the oven to 190°C/375°F/gas mark 5. Lightly grease and line 2 large baking sheets with nonstick baking parchment.

Cream together the butter and sugar in a large bowl. When the mixture has lightened slightly in colour add one egg, beat well, add the second egg and beat again. Don't worry if the mixture curdles slightly, just add 1 tablespoon of the flour and beat well. Sift together the flour, baking powder, salt and chilli powder and then stir into the creamed butter. Finally, stir the chopped dark chocolate into the mixture.

Spoon heaped tablespoons of the mixture, spaced well apart, on to the baking sheets, press down with dampened fingers to flatten slightly. Bake for 10–12 minutes or until the cookies begin to colour. Remove from the oven and allow to cool slightly on the baking sheets. Transfer to a wire rack.

To decorate, place the chocolate in a heatproof glass bowl set over a pan of gently simmering water, making sure that the bowl does not touch the water. It should take 2–3 minutes for the chocolate to melt, stir the chocolate well and remove it from the heat to cool for a couple of minutes. Dip a fork into the melted chocolate and drizzle over the cold cookies. Before the chocolate drizzle sets completely, scatter the cookies with a few chilli flakes.

with
a glass
of milk

Butterfly and Flower Cookies

Preparation time: 40 minutes
Cooking time: 7–8 minutes
Makes 24

75 g/3 oz/¾ cup unsalted butter, softened
75 g/3 oz/¾ cup caster (superfine) sugar
1 medium egg, at room temperature
½ teaspoon vanilla extract
250 g/8 oz/2 cups plain (all-purpose) flour, plus extra
    for dusting

To decorate
2–3 tablespoons icing (confectioners') sugar
375 g/12 oz/1½ cups pale blue regal icing
375 g/12 oz/1½ cups pale pink regal icing
2–3 tablespoons apricot jam, sieved

Preheat the oven to 180°C/350°F/gas mark 4. Grease and line 2–3 baking sheets with nonstick baking parchment.

Cream the butter and sugar together until pale and fluffy using a wooden spoon or electric hand whisk. Add the egg and vanilla extract and beat well – don't worry if the mixture curdles slightly, just beat in 1 tablespoon of the flour. Sift the flour and fold into the mixture until you have a stiff dough. If the dough seems too soft to roll out, refrigerate for 20 minutes.

Roll out the dough on a lightly floured cool surface until 2.5 mm/⅛ in thick. I find this is easiest to do between 2 sheets of clingfilm. Using butterfly- and flower-shaped cutters dusted with a little flour, or the stencils on page 89, cut out as many shapes as possible, as the more you have to reroll the dough, the tougher it will become. Using a metal palette knife or fish slice, carefully lift out the shapes and place on the baking sheets. Bake for 7–8 minutes or until the cookies start to turn a very pale golden colour. Transfer to a wire rack and leave to cool.

Once cool, you can decorate the cookies. Roll out the pale blue and pink icing separately on a cool surface dusted with a little icing sugar or between 2 sheets of clingfilm until 2.5 mm/⅛ in thick. Using the same shaped cutters as the cookies, dusted this time with a little icing sugar, cut out the same number of shapes. Using a clean paint brush, paint a little of the sieved jam on each cookie to ensure that the icing will stick, place the icing shapes on the cookies and press down lightly.

With the trimmings from the icing, make 6 currant-sized balls for each flower out of the pale blue regal icing, place them on the petals and flatten with dampened fingers. You could also place a ball in the centre of each flower if you wish. For each butterfly make 4 currant-sized balls of the pale pink icing, place them on the wings and press down with dampened fingertips to flatten. Take a slightly bigger piece of the pink icing and roll into a log shape slightly shorter than the length of the butterfly. Press down to form the body of the butterfly. Your cookies are now ready to enjoy. I guarantee they will fly off the plates.

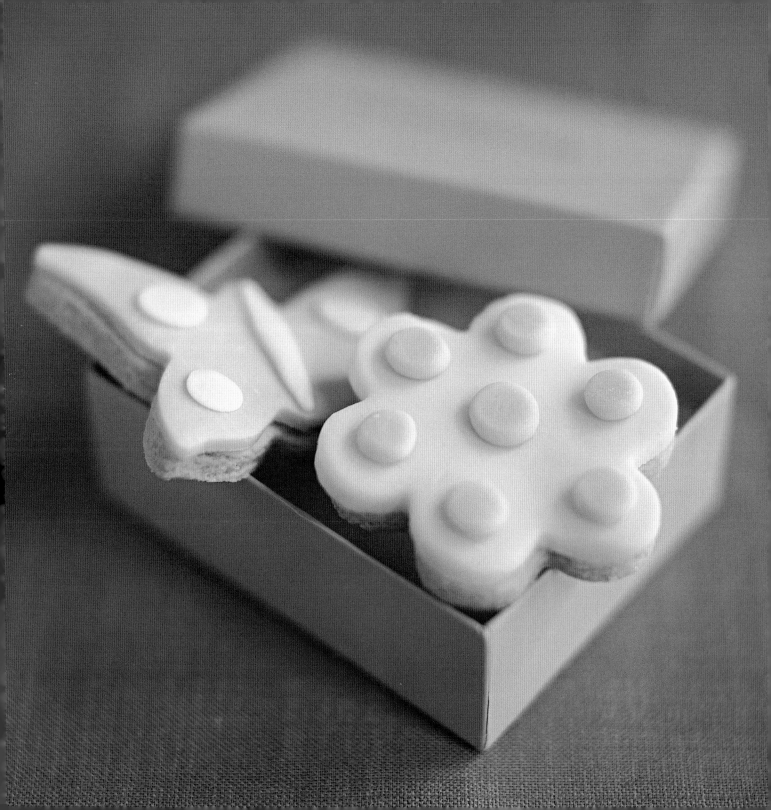

Marshmallow Rainbow Cookies

Preparation time: 40 minutes
Cooking time: 10 minutes
Chilling time: 20 minutes
Makes 16–20

90 g/3 oz/¾ cup unsalted butter, softened
90 g/3 oz/¾ cup caster (superfine) sugar
1 medium egg, at room temperature
½ teaspoon vanilla extract
250 g/8 oz/2 cups plain (all-purpose) flour

To decorate
150 g/5 oz/1 cup different coloured marshmallows

These pretty rainbow cookies are great fun and simple to make. The marshmallow becomes wonderfully sticky and chewy as it melts.

Preheat the oven to 180°C/350°F/gas mark 4. Grease and line 2–3 baking sheets with nonstick baking parchment.

Cream the butter and sugar together until pale and fluffy using a wooden spoon or electric hand whisk. Add the egg and vanilla extract and beat well – don't worry if the mixture curdles slightly, just beat in 1 tablespoon of the flour. Sift the flour and fold into the mixture until you have a stiff dough. If the dough seems too soft to roll, refrigerate for 20 minutes.

Roll out the dough on a lightly floured cool surface or between 2 sheets of clingfilm until 2.5 mm/⅛ in thick. Using a rainbow-shaped cookie cutter dusted with a little flour, cut out as many rainbows as possible, as the more you reroll the dough, the tougher it will become. If you don't have a rainbow-shaped cutter, just cut them out freehand using a knife, to a size of about 9 cm/3½ in wide. Using a metal palette knife or fish slice, carefully lift out the rainbows and place on the baking sheets. Bake for 8–9 minutes or until the cookies start to turn pale golden. Remove from the oven and arrange the mini marshmallows on the cookies in rainbow stripes. Cook for a further minute. Transfer to a wire rack to cool. Be careful, as the marshmallow will be very hot.

Face Cookies

Preparation time: 40 minutes
Cooking time: 5 minutes
Chilling time: up to 20 minutes
Makes 30

90 g/3 oz/¾ cup unsalted butter, softened
90 g/3 oz/¾ cup caster (superfine) sugar
1 medium egg, at room temperature
½ teaspoon vanilla extract
240 g/8 oz/2 cups plain (all-purpose) flour
2 tablespoons cocoa powder

To decorate
2–3 tablespoons icing (confectioners') sugar
375 g/12 oz/1½ cups pink or brown regal icing
2–3 tablespoons strawberry jam, sieved
a variety of edible icing pens

Preheat the oven to 180°C/350°F/gas mark 4. Grease and line 2 baking sheets with baking parchment.

Cream the butter and sugar together until pale and fluffy using a wooden spoon or electric hand whisk. Add the egg and vanilla extract and beat well. Remove 2 tablespoons of the flour and set aside. Sift the remaining flour and cocoa powder together and fold into the mixture until you have a stiff dough. If the dough seems too soft to roll out, refrigerate for 20 minutes.

Roll out the dough on a cool surface dusted with the reserved flour or between 2 sheets of clingfilm until 2.5mm/⅛ in thick. Using a 4–5 cm/1½–2 in diameter cookie cutter dusted with flour, cut out as many circles as possible, as the more you reroll the dough, the tougher it will become. Using a metal palette knife or fish slice, carefully lift out the circles and place on the baking sheets. Bake for 5 minutes. Transfer to a wire rack and leave to cool.

To decorate, roll out the regal icing on a cool surface dusted with a little icing sugar until 2.5 mm/⅛ in thick. Using the same cutter dusted with a little icing sugar, cut out the same number of circles. Stick the icing shapes to the cookies with a little jam. Use the icing pens to draw your smiley faces.

Dolphin Cookies

Preparation time: 25 minutes
Cooking time: 5–6 minutes
Chilling time: up to 20 minutes
Makes 25

90 g/3 oz/¾ cup unsalted butter, softened
90 g/3 oz/¾ cup caster (superfine) sugar
1 tablespoon runny honey
1 teaspoon finely grated orange zest
1 medium egg, at room temperature
½ teaspoon almond extract
250 g/8 oz/2 cups plain (all-purpose) flour, plus extra
   for dusting

To decorate
2–3 tablespoons icing (confectioners') sugar
375 g/12 oz/1½ cups silver blue regal icing
2–3 tablespoons marmalade, sieved
small candies for the eyes (optional)

The dolphin is such a simple, recognizable shape that it is very obviously a dolphin and therefore doesn't need much – if any – decoration. You can use any coloured small candy for the eyes.

Preheat the oven to 180°C/350°F/gas mark 4. Grease and line 2 baking sheets with nonstick baking parchment.

Beat the butter, sugar and honey together until pale and fluffy using a wooden spoon or electric hand whisk. Add the orange zest, egg and almond extract and beat well. Sift the flour and fold into the mixture until you have a stiff dough. If the dough seems too soft to roll out, refrigerate for 20 minutes.

Roll out the dough on a lightly floured cool surface or between 2 sheets of clingfilm until 2.5 mm/⅛ in thick. Using a 4–5 cm/1½–2 in dolphin-shaped cookie cutter dusted with a little flour or the stencil on page 89, cut out as many dolphins as possible, as the more you have to reroll the dough, the tougher it will become. Using a metal palette knife or fish slice, carefully lift out the dolphins and place on the baking sheets. Bake for 5–6 minutes. Transfer to a wire rack and leave to cool.

Once cool, you can decorate the cookies. Roll out the silver blue regal icing on a cool surface dusted with a little icing sugar or between 2 sheets of clingfilm until 2.5 mm/⅛ in thick. Using the same cutter as before, dusted this time with a little icing sugar, cut out the same number of dolphin shapes. Using a clean paintbrush, paint a little of the sieved marmalade on each cookie to ensure that the icing will stick, place the icing shapes on the cookies and press down lightly. Finish by giving each dolphin a candy eye if you wish.

Sugar and Spice and All Things Nice Cookies

Preparation time: 20 minutes
Cooking time: 10–12 minutes
Makes 24

60 g/2 oz/½ cup unsalted butter, softened
120 g/4 oz/1 cup light muscovado sugar
2 medium eggs, at room temperature
2 tablespoons milk
1 teaspoon vanilla extract
240 g/8 oz/2 cups plain (all-purpose) flour
1 teaspoon baking powder
½ teaspoon fine salt
1 teaspoon ground cinnamon
1 teaspoon ground ginger
½ teaspoon ground cloves
¼ teaspoon grated nutmeg

To decorate
2 tablespoons runny honey
2 tablespoons pink dust or sprinkles

These cookies are fantastic for a girls' party – it would be fun for the girls to be given the cookies so that they could decorate them themselves, or they could be given as a take-home gift. Edible pink dust or sprinkles are available from specialist cake shops and some larger supermarkets.

Preheat the oven to 180°C/350°F/gas mark 4. Grease and line 2 baking sheets with nonstick baking parchment.

Cream the butter and sugar together until fluffy and slightly paler in colour, using a wooden spoon or electric hand whisk. Add the eggs one at a time, beating them well each time, then add the milk and vanilla extract and beat well to incorporate. Sift the flour, baking powder, salt and spices together and fold into the mixture until you have a soft dough.

Roll the dough into golfball-sized balls, place on the baking sheets, leaving a space of 5 cm/2 in between each one, as they will spread when baking, and flatten with dampened fingers into 5 mm/⅛ in thick discs. Bake for 10–12 minutes or until the edges of the cookies just start to crisp. Transfer to a wire rack and leave to cool.

Once cool, warm the honey slightly so that it is runny enough to paint with. Using a clean paintbrush, paint the honey on the cookie in the shape of a heart or any simple shape, scatter the dust or sprinkles over the honey, shake off any excess and they are ready to eat.

Noughts and Crosses Cookies

Preparation time: 40 minutes
Cooking time: 5 minutes
Chilling time: up to 20 minutes
Makes 30

90 g/3 oz/¾ cup unsalted butter, softened
90 g/3 oz/¾ cup caster (superfine) sugar
1 medium egg, at room temperature
½ teaspoon vanilla extract
240 g/8 oz/2 cups plain (all-purpose) flour, plus extra
   for dusting

To decorate
2–3 tablespoons icing (confectioners') sugar
360 g/12 oz/1½ cups white regal icing
2–3 tablespoons apricot jam, sieved
30 g/1 oz/¼ cup black regal icing

My mother always told me never to play with my food but I think we can make an exception to the rule here! Mark out a noughts and crosses grid on either a blackboard as shown or a piece of card. There should be enough cookies for the winner to eat one of the opponent's cookies after each victory for quite a few games!

Preheat the oven to 180°C/350°F/gas mark 4. Grease and line 2 baking sheets with nonstick baking parchment.

Cream the butter and sugar together until pale and fluffy using a wooden spoon or electric hand whisk. Add the egg and vanilla extract and beat well – don't worry if the mixture curdles slightly, just beat in 1 tablespoon of the flour. Sift the flour and fold into the mixture until you have a stiff dough. If the dough seems too soft to roll out, refrigerate for 20 minutes.

Roll out the dough on a lightly floured cool surface or between 2 sheets of clingfilm until 2.5 mm/⅛ in thick. Using a 4–5 cm/1½–2 in diameter cookie cutter dusted with a little flour, cut out as many circles as possible, as the more you have to reroll the dough, the tougher it will become. Using a metal palette knife or fish slice, carefully lift out the circles and place on the baking sheets. Bake for 5 minutes or until the cookies start to turn a very pale golden colour. Transfer to a wire rack and leave to cool.

Once cool, you can decorate the cookies. Roll out the white regal icing on a cool surface dusted with a little icing sugar or between 2 sheets of clingfilm until 2.5 mm/⅛ in thick. Using the same cutter as before, dusted this time with a little icing sugar, cut out the same number of circles. Using a clean paintbrush, paint a little of the sieved jam on each cookie to ensure that the icing will stick, place the icing shapes on the cookies and press down lightly. Wipe the surface then roll out the black icing a little thinner than the white. Using a knife, carefully cut out 30 strips a little shorter than the width of the cookie and lay 2 strips over 15 of the cookies in a cross, pressing down to secure. Leave the remaining cookies plain white. Play can now commence – good luck!

Malteser Cookies

Preparation time: 20–25 minutes
Cooking time: 10–12 minutes
Makes 18

85 g/3 oz/½ cup unsalted butter, softened
170 g/6 oz/⅔ cup granulated sugar
1 egg
150 g/5 oz/1 heaped cup plain (all-purpose) flour
1 teaspoon baking powder
1 tablespoon cocoa powder
100 g/3½ oz/1 cup Maltesers, roughly chopped

To decorate
9 Maltesers, cut into halves (30 g/1 oz/¼ cup)

If Maltesers aren't your thing, or the box you bought is mysteriously empty, you could substitute the same quantity of milk (semi-sweet) chocolate and 2 tablespoons of Ovaltine (malted) drinking powder.

Preheat the oven to 180°C/350°F/gas mark 4. Grease and line 2 baking sheets with nonstick baking parchment.

Cream the butter and sugar together until pale and fluffy. Add the egg and beat for 1 minute until well incorporated. Sift the flour, baking powder and cocoa powder together and fold into the mixture, then add the Maltesers and stir until fully incorporated. Drop heaped tablespoons on to the baking sheets, leaving a 5 cm/2 in space between each one, as they will spread when baking, and flatten with lightly floured fingers into discs. Bake for 10–12 for minutes until the cookies turn golden around the edges.

To decorate, press a Malteser into each whilst still warm. Leave to cool on the baking sheets for 2 minutes before transferring to a wire rack. Serve at room temperature.

Toffee Apple Cookies

Preparation time: 15 minutes
Cooking time: 10–12 minutes
Makes 20

60 g/2 oz/½ cup unsalted butter, softened
60 g/2 oz/¼ cup soft brown sugar
120 g/4 oz/½ cup granulated sugar
1 egg
1 jar apple sauce (250 g/8 oz/1 cup)
175 g/6 oz/1½ cup plain (all-purpose) flour
1 teaspoon baking powder
90 g/3 oz/⅓ cup roughly chopped toffee

The pieces of toffee form the decoration because they come to the surface of the cookies as they melt when cooking. A delightful alternative to fairground toffee apples.

Preheat the oven to 200°C/400°F/gas mark 6. Grease 2 baking sheets with a little butter.

Cream the butter and sugars together until pale and fluffy using a wooden spoon or electric hand whisk. Add the egg, beating to incorporate before stirring in the apple sauce. Sift in the flour and baking powder and fold in to combine before mixing in the toffee pieces. The dough should be quite wet. Drop heaped tablespoons on to the prepared baking sheets, flattening down with dampened fingers. Bake for 10–12 minutes until the cookies turn golden around the edges. Leave to cool on the baking sheets for 2 minutes before transferring to a wire rack. Serve at room temperature.

Crunchy Bar Cookies

Preparation time: 25 minutes
Cooking time: 10–12 minutes
Makes 20

60 g/2 oz/½ cup unsalted butter, softened
120 g/4 oz/½ cup soft brown sugar
1 egg
180 g/6 oz/1½ cup plain (all-purpose) flour
1 teaspoon baking powder
1 tablespoon cocoa powder
85 g/3 oz/1 cup roughly chopped Crunchie (chocolate-
    coated honeycomb bar)

To decorate
35 g/1½ oz/¼ cup sliced Crunchie (chocolate-coated
    honeycomb bar)

These cookies are deliciously chewy because the honeycomb melts during the baking. However hard it is, do make sure you let the cookies cool down before eating them, as the honeycomb gets very hot.

Preheat the oven to 200°C/400°F/gas mark 6. Grease and line 2 baking sheets with nonstick baking parchment.

Cream the butter and sugar together until slightly paler in colour and fluffy. Add the egg and beat again until fully incorporated. Sift the flour, baking powder and cocoa powder together and fold into the mixture. Knead the Crunchie pieces into the dough. Roll the dough into golfball-sized balls, place on the baking sheets and flatten with dampened fingers into discs. Place 1 or 2 slices of the Crunchie in the centre of each cookie. Bake for 10–12 minutes until the cookies turn golden around the edges. Leave to cool on the baking sheets for 2 minutes before transferring to a wire rack. Serve at room temperature.

Mint Choc Chip Cookies

Preparation time: 25 minutes
Cooking time: 12 - 15 minutes
Makes 20

120 g/4 oz/½ cup unsalted butter, softened
60 g/2 oz/½ cup granulated sugar
60 g/1 oz/¼ cup soft brown sugar
a few drops of vanilla extract
1 medium egg, at room temperature
180 g/6 oz/1½ cups plain (all-purpose) flour
1 teaspoon baking powder
150 g/5 oz/1 cup mint chocolates

To decorate
10 mint chocolate cubes (50 g/1¾ oz/⅓ cup), halved

The combination of the chocolate and the refreshing mint in these cookies makes them wickedly moreish to anyone who loves After Eights (after-dinner mints).

Preheat the oven to 180°C/350°F/gas mark 4. Grease and line 2 baking sheets with nonstick baking parchment.

Cream the butter and sugars together until pale and fluffy. Add the egg and vanilla extract and beat for 1 minute until well mixed. Sift the flour and baking powder together and add to the mixture, gently folding in until fully incorporated. Roughly chop the mint chocolates and stir into the mixture. Drop heaped tablespoons on to the baking sheets, leaving a 5 cm/2 in space between each one, as they will spread when baking, and flatten with lightly floured fingers into discs. Bake for 5 minutes, then remove from the oven, place a half-piece of mint chocolate in the centre of each cookie and return to the oven for 7–10 minutes until the cookies turn golden around the edges. Leave to cool on the baking sheets for 2 minutes before transferring to a wire rack. Serve at room temperature.

Teddy Bear Cookies

Preparation time: 35 minutes
Cooking time: 7–8 minutes
Chilling time: 20 minutes
Makes 20–25

90 g/3 oz/¾ cup unsalted butter, softened
90 g/3 oz/¾ cup caster (superfine) sugar
1 medium egg, at room temperature
½ teaspoon vanilla extract
240 g/8 oz/2 cups plain (all-purpose) flour, plus extra
　　for dusting

To decorate
2–3 tablespoons icing (confectioners') sugar
360 g/12 oz/1½ cups light brown regal icing
2–3 tablespoons apricot jam, sieved
3 tablespoons small pink candy balls
1 black edible icing pen

Edible icing marker pens are available from specialist cake shops and are a brilliant way to decorate cakes as well as cookies. They also come in a wide variety of colours.

Preheat the oven to 180°C/350°F/gas mark 4. Grease and line 2–3 baking sheets with nonstick baking parchment.

Cream the butter and sugar together until pale and fluffy using a wooden spoon or electric hand whisk. Add the egg and vanilla extract and beat well – don't worry if the mixture curdles slightly, just beat in 1 tablespoon of the flour. Sift the flour and fold into the mixture until you have a stiff dough. If the dough seems too soft to roll out, refrigerate for 20 minutes.

Roll out the dough on a lightly floured cool surface or between 2 sheets of clingfilm until 2.5 mm (⅛ in) thick. Using a teddy bear-shaped cookie cutter dusted with a little flour, cut out as many bears as possible, as the more you have to reroll the dough, the tougher it will become. Using a metal palette knife or fish slice, carefully lift out the cats and place on the baking sheets. Bake for 7–8 minutes or until the cookies start to turn a very pale golden colour. Transfer to a wire rack and leave to cool.

Once cool, you can decorate the cookies. Roll out the light brown regal icing on a cool surface dusted with a little icing sugar or between 2 sheets of clingfilm until 2.5 mm/⅛ in thick. Using the same cutter as before, dusted this time with a little icing sugar, cut out the same number of bear shapes. Using a clean paintbrush, paint a little of the sieved jam on each cookie to ensure that the icing will stick, place the icing shapes on the cookies and press down lightly. Decorate the bears with the pink candy as paws and buttons, pressing down so that they don't fall off. Finish by carefully drawing on eyes, noses and mouths with the black icing pen.

Draw your own Picture

Preparation time: up to 45 minutes
Cooking time: 5 minutes
Chilling time: up to 20 minutes
Makes 30

90 g/3 oz/¾ cup unsalted butter, softened
90 g/3 oz/¾ cup caster (superfine) sugar
1 medium egg, at room temperature
½ teaspoon vanilla extract
250 g/8 oz/2 cups plain (all-purpose) flour, plus extra
   for dusting

To decorate
2–3 tablespoons icing (confectioners') sugar
360 g/12 oz/1½ cups white regal icing
2–3 tablespoons apricot jam, sieved
a variety of edible icing pens

This is a lovely way to keep children amused at a birthday party and they can all decorate their own cookies to take home with them.

Preheat the oven to 180°C/350°F/gas mark 4. Grease and line 2 baking sheets with nonstick baking parchment.

Cream the butter and sugar together until pale and fluffy using a wooden spoon or electric hand whisk. Add the egg and vanilla extract and beat well – don't worry if the mixture curdles slightly, just beat in 1 tablespoon of the flour. Sift the flour and fold into the mixture until you have a stiff dough. If the dough seems too soft to roll out, refrigerate for 20 minutes.

Roll out the dough on a lightly floured cool surface or between 2 sheets of clingfilm until 2.5 mm/⅛ in thick. Using a 4–5 cm/1½–2 in diameter cookie cutter dusted with a little flour, cut out as many circles as possible, as the more you have to reroll the dough, the tougher it will become. Using a metal palette knife or fish slice, carefully lift out the circles and place on the baking sheets. Bake for 5 minutes or until the cookies start to turn a very pale golden colour. Transfer to a wire rack and leave to cool.

Once cool, you can decorate the cookies. Roll out the white regal icing on a cool surface dusted with a little icing sugar or between 2 sheets of clingfilm until 2.5 mm/⅛ in thick. Using the same cutter as before, dusted this time with a little icing sugar, cut out the same number of circles. Using a clean paintbrush, paint a little of the sieved jam on each cookie to ensure that the icing will stick, place the icing shapes on the cookies and press down lightly. Give the children the edible icing pens and let them draw their own pictures on the icing – simple designs tend to work best.

Car Cookies

Preparation time: 35 minutes
Cooking time: 5–8 minutes
Chilling time: 1 hour
Makes 25–30

60 g/2 oz/½ cup unsalted butter, softened
240 g/8 oz/2 cups plain (all-purpose) flour
90 g/3 oz/½ cup brown sugar
3–4 tablespoons golden syrup
1 medium egg, at room temperature, lightly beaten
    (you will only need to use half)
1 teaspoon finely grated lemon zest
½ teaspoon mixed spice
½ teaspoon ground ginger
¼ teaspoon bicarbonate of soda (baking soda)
pinch of fine salt
extra flour for rolling

To decorate
2 tablespoons icing (confectioners') sugar
360 g/12 oz/1½ cups of your favourite coloured regal icing
2 tablespoons apricot jam, sieved
60 g/2 oz/½ cup black regal icing

You can choose any of your favourite colours to decorate the cars, but I find that primary colours tend to look best. If you have lots of bits of leftover icing, you can make a whole range of different coloured cars.

Preheat the oven to 190°C/375°F/gas mark 5. Grease and line 2 baking sheets with nonstick baking parchment.

Cream the butter until smooth. Add half of the flour with the sugar, syrup, half of the egg, lemon zest, spices, bicarbonate of soda and salt. Beat until smooth using a wooden spoon or electric hand whisk on a low speed. Stir in the remaining flour and knead for 30 seconds until you have a smooth dough. Wrap the dough in clingfilm and refrigerate for 1 hour.

Roll out the dough on a lightly floured cool surface or between 2 sheets of clingfilm until 5 mm/¼ in thick. Using a car-shaped cookie cutter dusted with a little flour or the stencil on page 91, cut out as many cars as possible, as you more you have to reroll the dough, the tougher it will become. Using a metal palette knife or fish slice, carefully lift out the cars and place on the baking sheets. Bake for 5–8 minutes until the cookies are just starting to colour around the edges. Leave to cool on the baking sheets for 2 minutes before transferring to a wire rack to cool completely.

Once cool, you can decorate the cookies. Roll out the chosen icing on a cool surface dusted with a little icing sugar or between 2 sheets of clingfilm until 2.5 mm/⅛ in thick. Using the same cutter as before, dusted this time with a little icing sugar, cut out the same number of car shapes. Using a clean paintbrush, paint a little of the sieved jam on each cookie to ensure that the icing will stick, place the icing shapes on the cookies and press down lightly. Clean the surfaces before rolling out the black icing for the wheels; it should be a little thinner than the coloured icing. Using a tiny cookie cutter or the fat end of a small piping nozzle, cut out the small round wheels. Carefully lift out the wheels and place two on each car, pressing down lightly to secure, as you don't want your wheels to fall off.

with a glass of milk

44

Gingerbread Family

Preparation time: 25 minutes
Chilling time: 1 hour
Cooking time: 6–8 minutes adults, 5 minutes children
Makes 8–9 families

120 g/4 oz/1 cup unsalted butter, softened
480 g/16 oz/4 cups plain (all-purpose) flour
180 g/6 oz/1 cup brown sugar
60 g/2 oz/¼ cup black treacle (molasses) or golden syrup
1 medium egg, at room temperature
1 tablespoon finely grated orange zest
1 teaspoon mixed spice
1 teaspoon ground ginger
½ teaspoon bicarbonate of soda (baking soda)
¼ teaspoon fine salt
extra flour for rolling

To decorate
1 small tube of white writing icing

Preheat the oven to 190°C/375°F/gas mark 5. Grease and line 3–4 baking sheets with nonstick baking parchment.

Cream the butter until smooth, then add half of the flour with the sugar, treacle or syrup, egg, orange zest, spices, bicarbonate of soda and salt. Beat until smooth using a wooden spoon or electric hand whisk on a low speed. Stir in the remaining flour and knead for 30 seconds until you have smooth dough. Wrap the dough in clingfilm and refrigerate for 1 hour.

Roll out the dough on a lightly floured surface until 5mm/¼ in thick; you may need to do this in 2 batches, depending on the size of your surface. Using cookie cutters lightly dusted in flour, or the stencils on page 90, cut out as many figures as possible. Place on the baking sheets, leaving a space between each figure; depending on the size of your oven, you may have to bake them in batches. Bake for 6–8 minutes (the small figures will need only 5 minutes). Leave to cool on the baking sheets before transferring to a wire rack to cool completely.

To decorate, pipe on noses, eyes and buttons as desired. Leave to set for 2 minutes before serving.

Peanut Butter Cookies

Preparation time: 15 minutes
Cooking time: 25–30 minutes
Makes 25–30

120 g/4 oz/½ cup crunchy peanut butter
finely grated zest of half an orange
60 g/2 oz/¼ cup caster (superfine) sugar
3–4 tablespoons light brown sugar
60 g/2 oz/½ cup unsalted butter, softened
1 medium egg
120 g/4 oz/1 cup plain (all-purpose) flour
1 teaspoon baking powder

To decorate
60 g/2 oz/½ cup peanuts
2 tablespoons golden syrup

I prefer the crunchy peanut butter for these cookies, but if you are more of a smoothie feel free to use the smooth instead.

Preheat the oven to 150°C/300°F/gas mark 2. Grease and line 2 baking sheets with nonstick baking parchment.

Beat the peanut butter, orange zest, sugars and butter together until light and fluffy using a wooden spoon or electric hand whisk. Beat in the egg, then, once incorporated, gently fold in the flour and baking powder. Gather the mixture together into a ball and knead for a moment until you have a fairly firm dough. Roll the dough into ping-pong ball-sized balls, place on the baking sheets spaced well apart and flatten with dampened fingers into Frisbee-shaped cookies. Bake for 15 minutes.

Meanwhile, roughly chop the peanuts and mix with the syrup so that all the peanuts are evenly coated. Spoon a teaspoon of the nut mixture in the centre of each cookie, then return to the oven for a further 10 minutes. Leave to cool on the baking sheets for 2–3 minutes before transferring to a wire rack to cool. They are also delicious served warm.

Family Hands Cookies

Preparation time: 35 minutes
Chilling time: 1 hour
Cooking time: 5–8 minutes
Makes 10–15

60 g/2 oz/½ cup unsalted butter, softened
240 g/8 oz/2 cups plain (all-purpose) flour
90 g/3 oz/½ cup brown sugar
3–4 tablespoons golden syrup
1 medium egg, at room temperature, lightly beaten (you
    will only need to use half)
½ tablespoon finely grated orange zest
½ teaspoon mixed spice
½ teaspoon ground ginger
¼ teaspoon bicarbonate of soda (baking soda)
pinch of fine salt
Extra flour for rolling

To decorate
2 tablespoons icing (confectioners') sugar
360 g/12 oz/1½ cups pale pink or brown icing
2 tablespoons apricot jam, sieved

Get the whole family involved with these cookies by getting everyone to draw round their hands. You can then have fun guessing whose is whose when they are finished and decorated.

Preheat the oven to 190°C/375°F/gas mark 5. Grease and line 2 baking sheets with nonstick baking parchment.

Cream the butter until smooth. Add half of the flour with the sugar, syrup, half of the egg, orange zest, spices, bicarbonate of soda and salt. Beat until smooth using a wooden spoon or electric hand whisk. Stir in the remaining flour and knead for 30 seconds until you have smooth dough. Wrap the dough in clingfilm and refrigerate for 1 hour.

Meanwhile, draw round your hands on a piece of tracing paper and carefully cut out hand stencils.

Roll out the dough on a lightly floured cool surface or between 2 sheets of clingfilm until 3 mm/¼ in thick. Lay the cut-out hands on the dough and, using a small knife, carefully cut round them (don't throw away the stencils as you will need them for the icing). Using a metal palette knife or fish slice, carefully lift out the hand shapes and place on the baking sheets, leaving a 2.5 cm/1 in space between each hand. Bake for 5–8 minutes, depending on the size of the hands. Leave to cool on the baking sheets for 2 minutes before transferring to a wire rack to cool completely.

Once cool, you can decorate the cookies. Roll out the chosen icing on a cool surface dusted with a little icing sugar or between 2 sheets of clingfilm until 2.5 mm/⅛ in thick. Using the hand stencils, cut out the hands in the same way as before. Using a clean paintbrush, paint a little of the sieved jam on each cookie to ensure that the icing will stick, place the icing shapes on the cookies and press down lightly. You could also mark out knuckles by gently scoring the icing with a skewer, and add nails by making indents with the handle end of a spoon or your fingertip.

with an
aperitif

Fennel and Parmesan Cookies

Preparation time: 15–20 minutes
Cooking time: 8–10 minutes
Makes 14–16

50 g/2 oz/1 cup finely grated Parmesan cheese
50 g/2 oz/¼ cup unsalted butter, softened
2 teaspoons fennel seeds
70 g/2½ oz/½ cup plain (all-purpose) flour
pinch of fine salt

To decorate
1 tablespoon fennel seeds

Fennel seeds have a similar aniseed flavour to the feathery tops of a fennel bulb and when combined with the Parmesan they make these cookies a delicious treat. Serving them with chilled Italian dry white wine brings out the Italian connection.

Preheat the oven to 200°C/400°F/gas mark 6. Grease and line 2 baking sheets with nonstick baking parchment.

Beat the Parmesan and butter together with a wooden spoon until smooth and well combined. Grind the fennel seeds in a pestle and mortar, add to the mixture with the flour and salt and stir until all the flour is combined. Don't be tempted to add any liquid because the dough should be reasonably dry. Gather the dough into a ball and knead for 1 minute or until you have a smooth ball. Roll the dough into marble-sized balls, place on the baking sheets and flatten with dampened fingers into 5 mm/¼ inch discs. Scatter over the fennel seeds and press in slightly. Bake for 8–10 minutes or until the cookies are golden.

Either transfer to a wire rack to cool or serve them straight from the oven, as they are especially delicious served hot. If you are making these in advance, it is best to leave them to cool completely before storing them in an airtight container.

Rosemary and Sun-Dried Tomato Cookies

Preparation time: 40 minutes
Cooking time: 10 minutes
Makes 30–35

150 g/4½ oz/¾ cup diced unsalted butter, cold
150 g/5 oz/1¼ cups plain (all purpose) flour
1 tablespoon finely chopped fresh rosemary
1 tablespoon sun-dried tomato purée (paste)
1 teaspoon fine salt
1 teaspoon freshly ground black pepper

Sun-dried tomato purée is now widely available in larger supermarkets – you should find it in the aisle with other tomato purées and canned tomatoes. It is a useful thing to keep in the fridge and use to liven up sandwich fillings and many Mediterranean dishes, and it should keep for up to a month.

Place all the ingredients in a food processor and pulse until the mixture resembles fine breadcrumbs. Be careful not to overwork the flour, as it will toughen the dough. If you don't have a food processor, rub the butter into the flour until the mixture resembles fine breadcrumbs, then stir in the remaining ingredients. Gather the dough into a ball, wrap in clingfilm and refrigerate for 30 minutes.

Preheat the oven to 200°C/400°F/gas mark 6. Grease and line 2–3 baking sheets with nonstick baking parchment.

Roll out the dough on a lightly floured cool surface into a large circle 2.5 mm/⅛ in thick. I find this is easiest to do between 2 sheets of clingfilm. Using a 2.5 cm/1 in diameter cutter, cut out 30–35 discs, place on the baking sheets and bake for 8–10 minutes. Transfer to a wire rack and leave to cool completely before serving or storing in an airtight container.

Aromatic Thyme and Lemon Cookies

Preparation time: 15–20 minutes
Cooking time: 8–10 minutes
Makes 14–16

100 g/4 oz/1 cup finely grated mild Cheddar cheese
50 g/2 oz/¼ cup unsalted butter, softened
2 tablespoons fresh thyme leaves, bruised
finely grated zest of 1 lemon
pinch of fine salt
¼ teaspoon coarse ground black pepper
60 g/2½ oz/½ cup plain (all-purpose) flour

To decorate
a few sprigs of thyme

Bruising the thyme leaves will help release the aromatic essential oils, giving your cookies a wonderful aroma and flavour. If you would prefer to use lemon thyme in this recipe, you should reduce the amount of lemon zest to that of half a lemon.

Preheat the oven to 200°C/400°F/gas mark 6. Grease and line 2 baking sheets with nonstick baking parchment.

 Beat the Cheddar and butter together with a wooden spoon until well mixed. Stir in the thyme leaves, lemon zest, salt and black pepper before adding the flour. Continue to stir the mixture until it forms a soft dough with all the ingredients well mixed in. It may be easier to gather the dough with your hands and knead for 30 seconds–1 minute. Roll the dough into marble-sized balls, place on the baking sheets and flatten with dampened fingers into discs. Bake for 8–10 minutes until a light golden brown in colour. Leave to cool on the baking sheets before transferring to a wire rack. Alternatively, if serving hot, transfer to a warm serving plate, decorated with scattered thyme sprigs – if you can find them, the sprigs with small purplish flowers are especially pretty.

Green Olive and Chilli Cookies

Preparation time: 15–20 minutes
Cooking time: 8–10 minutes
Makes 24

55 g/2 oz/½ cup grated Cheddar cheese, at room temperature
120 g/4 oz/1 cup butter, softened
1/4 teaspoon coarse ground black pepper
55 g/2 oz/½ cup plain (all-purpose) flour
25 g/1 oz/¼ cup pitted green olives, finely chopped
1½ teaspoons finely chopped red chilli, seeds removed

To decorate
6 green pitted olives

If you have a glass with a pattern on the base, you can press it into the top of the cookies to leave an indented pattern. If you can find pimento-stuffed olives, they look and taste great on top of the cookies as decoration.

Preheat the oven to 200°C/400°F/gas mark 6. Grease and line 2 baking sheets with nonstick baking parchment.

 Beat the Cheddar and butter together with a wooden spoon until smooth and well combined. Stir in the black pepper, flour and olives and gather the mixture into a ball with your hands. Knead gently for approximately 1 minute until all the flour is incorporated. Roll the dough into marble-sized balls, place on the baking sheets and flatten with dampened fingers or the flat base of a glass dipped in flour into 5 mm/¼ in discs. Slice each olive into 4 and place a slice in the centre of each disc. Bake for 8–10 minutes or until the cookies are golden brown on top.

 You can either serve these cookies warm or leave to cool on a wire rack and serve at room temperature.

Oregano and Red Pepper Cookies

Preparation time: 15–20 minutes
Cooking time: 8–10 minutes
Makes 14–16

1 red bell pepper (capsicum)
100 g/4 oz/1 cup finely grated mild Cheddar cheese
50 g/2 oz/¼ cup unsalted butter, softened
2 teaspoons fresh chopped oregano
pinch of fine salt
1 teaspoon black pepper
60 g/2½ oz/½ cup plain (all-purpose) flour

To decorate
a few sprigs of oregano

If you like pizza, you will love the taste of these yummy bite-sized cookies, with all the flavours of a pizza but without the dough so you will have plenty of room left for a meal afterwards.

Preheat the oven to 200°C/400°F/gas mark 6. Grease and line 2 baking sheets with nonstick baking parchment.

Place the red pepper on a baking sheet and bake in the preheated oven for 20 minutes or until the skin of has blackened slightly. Remove from the oven and place in a plastic bag (or bowl covered with clingfilm) until cool.

Meanwhile, beat the Cheddar and butter together with a wooden spoon until fully combined and smooth. Remove the cooled pepper from the bag or bowl and remove the core, seeds and skin. Finely chop the flesh, drain away any excess liquid and add to the butter and cheese mixture with the oregano, salt and black pepper. Stir in the flour until fully incorporated and knead for 30 seconds until smooth but slightly sticky. Roll the dough into walnut-sized balls, place on the baking sheets and flatten with dampened fingers into 5 mm/¼ in discs. Bake for 8–10 minutes.

Leave to cool on the baking sheet for 1 minute before transferring to a wire rack. Serve either warm or at room temperature. Decorate the plate with sprigs of fresh oregano.

Marmite Cookies

Preparation time: 15–20 minutes
Cooking time: 8 minutes
Makes 14–16

100 g/3½ oz/1 cup finely grated mild Cheddar cheese
50 g/2 oz/¼ cup unsalted butter, softened
2 tablespoons Marmite
pinch of fine salt
¼ teaspoon freshly ground black pepper
60 g/2½ oz/½ cup plain (all-purpose) flour

To decorate
2 tablespoons flaked almonds

I am a big fan of Marmite but people tend to either love it or hate it. If you come into the latter category, you probably won't be reading any further! A tip for accurately measuring Marmite or anything sticky is to rub a little cooking oil on to the measuring spoon before measuring, as this will enable the Marmite to glide off easily.

Preheat the oven to 200°C/400°F/gas mark 6. Grease and line 2 baking sheets with nonstick baking parchment.

Beat the Cheddar and butter together with a wooden spoon until well mixed and smooth. Stir in the Marmite, salt and black pepper and continue to stir until all the ingredients have been incorporated. Tip in the flour and combine as best you can before gathering the dough with your hands and kneading for 30 seconds to form a slightly sticky ball. If the dough is too sticky, lightly sprinkle some flour on your hands before rolling the dough into 14–16 even walnut-sized balls. Place on the baking sheets, flatten slightly with floured fingers and place a flaked almond on each one to decorate. Bake for 8–10 minutes. Leave to cool on the baking sheets for 3–4 minutes before transferring to a wire rack to cool completely.

with an aperitif

Parmesan and Cayenne Crisps

Preparation time: 40 minutes
Cooking time: 8-10 minutes
Makes 35–40

125 g/4 oz/¾ cup butter, softened
110g/4 oz/¾ cup plain (all-purpose) flour
25 g/1 oz/½ cup finely grated Parmesan cheese
½ teaspoon cayenne pepper
½ teaspoon black pepper

To decorate
1 tablespoon grated Parmesan cheese
½ teaspoon cayenne pepper

These delicate little crisps are great to have on their own as a savoury snack or to have with drinks before a dinner party. They can be prepared in advance; just roll and cut them out and freeze on trays, then when you are ready to serve them you can pop them in the oven straight from the freezer and they will be ready in no time.

Grease 2 baking sheets and line them with nonstick baking parchment.

Place all the ingredients in a food processor and pulse until the mixture resembles fine breadcrumbs. Alternatively, you can rub the butter, flour and Parmesan with your fingers until the mixture resembles fine breadcrumbs, then stir in the cayenne pepper and black pepper. Gather the mixture together with your hands to form a dough. Try not to overhandle the dough, as you will overwork the flour and end up with tough cookies. Wrap in clingfilm and refrigerate for 30 minutes or until hard.

Preheat the oven to 200°C/400°F/gas mark 6.

Roll out the dough on a lightly floured cool surface into a rectangle 5mm/¼ in thick. Using a cutter or the blade of a sharp knife, cut out rectangles 5 x 1cm/½ x 2 in and place on the baking sheets. Bake for 8–10 minutes or until the crisps are golden brown. Leave to cool slightly on the baking sheet before carefully transferring to a wire rack to cool completely. Don't be heavyhanded with the cookies as they are quite fragile.

Cheddar and Chive Cookies

Preparation time: 25 minutes
Cooking time: 10 minutes
Makes 24

110 g/4 oz/1 cup grated Cheddar cheese, at room temperature
50 g/2 oz/¼ cup butter, softened
1 teaspoon prepared mustard, preferably English
¼ teaspoon ground black pepper
pinch of fine salt
50 g/2 oz/½ cup plain (all-purpose) flour
1 tablespoon snipped chives

To decorate
1 tablespoon white mustard seeds

If chives are unavailable, you can substitute finely chopped green tops of spring onions (scallions) or even – for a completely different flavour – chopped parsley.

Preheat the oven 200°C/400°F/gas mark 6. Line 2 baking sheets with nonstick baking parchment.

Beat the Cheddar and butter together until smooth and combined, then stir in the mustard, black pepper and salt. Sift the flour and tip into the cheese and butter with the snipped chives, then gather into a ball with your hands. Knead gently for approximately 1 minute until all the flour is incorporated. Don't tempted to add any liquid – it will come together with the heat of your hands. Roll the dough into marble-sized balls, place on the baking sheets and flatten with dampened fingers into 5 mm/¼ in discs. Sprinkle over the mustard seeds and press in slightly. Bake for 8–10 minutes until the cookies are golden brown.

I like to serve these straight from the oven but if you are making them in advance it is best to transfer them to a wire rack to cool completely before storing them in an airtight container. To warm them through when serving, place them in an oven preheated to 180°C/350°F/gas mark 4 for 5 minutes.

Jalapeño Cornbread Cookies

Preparation time: 40 minutes
Cooking time: 15 minutes
Chilling time: 30 minutes
Makes 50

200 g/7 oz/1 cup cold unsalted butter
100 g/3½ oz/½ cup plain (all-purpose) flour
70 g/2¼ oz/½ cup coarse cornmeal
½ teaspoon fine salt
½ teaspoon freshly ground black pepper
50 g/2 oz/⅓ cup pickled green chillies (jalapeños), thinly sliced

To decorate
3 pickled green chillies (jalapeños)
finely grated zest of 1 lime

These little savoury cookies are a terrific treat to serve with drinks. They melt in your mouth and the chilli gives them that added kick.

Dice the butter and place in a food processor. Sift the flour, cornmeal and salt together, tip into the food processor with the black pepper and chillies, and pulse until the mixture resembles fine breadcrumbs. If you don't have a food processor, you can rub the butter into the flour using your fingers. Gather the mixture together into a ball, wrap in clingfilm and refrigerate for 30 minutes.

Preheat the oven to 200°C/400°F/gas mark 6. Grease and line 2 nonstick baking sheets with baking parchment.

Roll out the dough on a lightly floured cool surface until 5 mm/¼ in thick. I find this is easiest to do between 2 sheets of clingfilm. Cut out 2.5 cm/1 in diameter discs (if you don't have the right cutter, you can use the thicker end of a large piping nozzle). Transfer to the baking sheets and bake for 15 minutes or until the cookies are golden.

To decorate, top the cookies with thinly sliced chillies and lime zest and serve either warm or at room temperature.

Sesame Seed Cookies

Preparation time: 15–20 minutes
Cooking time: 8–10 minutes
Makes 14–16

1 tablespoon sesame seeds
2 tablespoons rolled oats
50 g/2 oz/½ cup grated mild Cheddar cheese
50 g/2 oz/¼ cup unsalted butter, softened
½ teaspoon black pepper
pinch of fine salt
50 g/1¾ oz/⅓ cup plain (all-purpose) flour

To decorate
2 tablespoons sesame seeds

Sesame seeds are a favourite ingredient in savoury cookies. Their flavour, which is enhanced by roasting them, is subtle and this makes them suitable to eat with most drinks and before many types of food.

Preheat the oven to 200°C/400°F/gas mark 6. Grease and line 2 baking sheets with nonstick greaseproof parchment.

Roast the sesame seeds and oats in the preheated oven for 10 minutes or until the sesame seeds are light golden.

Beat the Cheddar and butter together until smooth and well mixed. Stir in the toasted sesame seeds with the oats, black pepper and salt and mix well before adding the flour. Continue stirring until all the flour is combined and the mixture has formed a dry dough. Gather the dough together with your hands and knead for 30 seconds until smooth, then roll into marble-sized balls. Spread out the sesame seeds for decorating on a plate or small tray, roll each dough ball in the sesame seeds, flatten in your hands into 5 mm/¼ in discs and place on the baking sheets. Bake for 8–10 minutes. Leave to cool on the baking sheets for 2 minutes before transferring to a wire rack. Serve at room temperature.

Mustard Nibbles

Preparation time: 40 minutes
Cooking time: 10 minutes
Chilling time: 30 minutes
Makes 30–35

150 g/4½ oz/¾ cup unsalted butter, cold
150 g/4½ oz/¾ cup plain (all-purpose) flour
2 tablespoons English mustard
1 teaspoon fine salt
1 teaspoon freshly ground black pepper
1 tablespoon black mustard seeds

These tiny cookies are a fantastic savoury treat, perfect to have before spicy food or even just with drinks. I love them with an ice-cold beer.

Place all the ingredients except the mustard seeds in a food processor and pulse 5 or 6 times – if you overmix, the mixture will become tough. When it resembles fine breadcrumbs, remove and gather together into a ball, then wrap in clingfilm and refrigerate for 30 minutes.

Preheat the oven to 200°C/400°F/gas mark 6. Grease and line 2–3 baking sheets with nonstick baking parchment.

Roll out the dough on a lightly floured surface until 2.5 mm/⅛ in thick, then sprinkle with the reserved mustard seeds. Cut into 2.5 cm/1 in fluted diamond shapes (if you don't have such a cutter, use any small shape). Place on the baking sheets and bake for 7–10 minutes. Serve immediately or at room temperature.

Peppery Poppy Seed Cookies

Preparation time: 15–20 minutes
Cooking time: 8–10 minutes
Makes 14–16

50 g/2 oz/½ cup grated mild Cheddar cheese,
   at room temperature
50 g/2 oz/¼ cup unsalted butter, softened
2 teaspoons poppy seeds
1 teaspoon black pepper
pinch of fine salt
50 g/2 oz/⅓ cup plain (all-purpose) flour

To decorate
2 tablespoons poppy seeds

It is important to have the Cheddar and butter at room temperature to enable you to mix them thoroughly. I recommend using a mild Cheddar, as a strong variety would overpower the flavour of the poppy seeds and its purpose is to bind the cookie together rather than be a primary flavour.

Preheat the oven to 200°C/400°F/gas mark 6. Grease and line 2 baking sheets with nonstick baking parchment.

Beat the Cheddar and butter together with a wooden spoon until well mixed and smooth. Stir in the poppy seeds, black pepper and salt before stirring in the flour. Keep stirring until the flour is fully incorporated. Gather the mixture together in your hands and knead until you have a soft, smooth dough. Roll the dough into marble-sized balls and place on the baking sheets leaving a 5 cm/2 in space between each one, as they will spread when baking. Flatten them with dampened fingers into 2.5 mm/⅛ in discs. Sprinkle over the poppy seeds and bake for 8–10 minutes or until the cookies are starting to brown around the edges. They will need to cool and harden on the baking sheets for a while before you are able to move them. Transfer to a wire rack and serve at room temperature.

with a clear
conscience

Banana Bran Cookies

Preparation time: 15 minutes
Cooking time: 15–17 minutes
Makes 12

120 g/4 oz/1 cup plain (all-purpose) flour
65 g/2 oz/½ cup rolled oats
5 tablespoons natural bran
½ teaspoon baking powder
60 g/2 oz/½ cup unsalted butter, plus extra for greasing
1 tablespoon golden syrup
3 medium or 4 small ripe bananas
3 tablespoons low fat natural (plain) yogurt

To decorate
3 tablespoons natural bran

Bran is well known to be a good source of fibre, while bananas are rich in potassium, which helps to regulate blood pressure and the heartrate. Altogether a guilt-free pleasure.

Preheat the oven to 180°C/350°F/gas mark 4. Grease 2 baking sheets with butter.

Mix the flour, oats, 3 tablespoons of the bran and baking powder together.
Melt the butter in a small pan with the syrup and quickly stir into the dry ingredients. Mash the bananas with a fork in a separate bowl and stir into the mixture with the yogurt until you have a very sticky dough. Sprinkle the remaining 2 tablespoons of bran over each greased baking sheet. Using a dessertspoon, drop spoonfuls on to the baking sheets, leaving a 5 cm/2 in space between each one, as they will spread when baking. Flatten with dampened fingers into 5 mm/¼ in thick discs and sprinkle with the remaining 3 tablespoons of bran, making sure that each disc is evenly coated. Bake for 15–17 minutes until golden brown.

Leave to cool on the baking sheets for 2 minutes before transferring to a wire rack to cool completely. These are also delicious served warm.

Apricot and Honey Cookies Dipped in Yogurt Icing

Preparation time: 20 minutes
Cooking time: 10 minutes
Makes 20–22

120 g/4 oz/1 cup unsalted butter, softened
175 g/6 oz/1 cup golden caster (superfine) sugar
3 tablespoons runny honey
2 eggs, at room temperature
240 g/8 oz/2 cups plain (all-purpose) flour
1 teaspoon baking powder
½ teaspoon fine salt
200 g/7 oz/1 cup whole dried apricots, roughly chopped

To decorate
240 g/8 oz/2 cups icing (confectioners') sugar, sifted
2 tablespoons fat-free vanilla yogurt
1 tablespoon lemon or lime juice
1 teaspoon finely grated zest of 1 lemon or lime

The icing on this cookie may seem a little decadent for a healthy cookie but a little goes a long way, and the yogurt is fat-free. However, if you are feeling particularly virtuous, you can leave out the icing.

Preheat the oven to 160°C/325°F/gas mark 3. Grease and line 2 baking sheets with nonstick baking parchment.

Cream the butter, sugar and honey together until paler in colour and smooth using an electric hand whisk. Add the eggs one at a time. Sift the flour, baking powder and salt together and fold into the mixture. Knead the apricots into the dough, taking care not to overknead. Spoon heaped tablespoons on to the baking sheets, leaving a 5 cm/2 in space between each and flatten into 5 mm/¼ in thick discs. Bake for 10 minutes. Leave to cool on the baking sheets.

To decorate, mix all the icing ingredients together, making sure that you beat out any lumps. Don't be tempted to add any more liquid – the mixture will get quite runny. Dip half of each cold cookie into the icing mixture and leave to set.

Carrot and Orange Cookies

Preparation time: 20 minutes
Cooking time: 10–12 minutes
Makes 16–18

60 g/2 oz/½ cup unsalted butter
1 tablespoon golden syrup
2 medium carrots
finely grated zest of 1 orange
120 g/4 oz/1 cup plain (all-purpose) flour
15 g/½ oz/½ cup natural bran
60 g/2 oz/¼ cup soft dark brown sugar

To decorate
2 tablespoons of finely chopped candied orange peel

Candied peel is widely available in large supermarkets. It lasts for months and is handy for many dishes other than traditional Christmas cakes.

Preheat the oven to 220°C/425°F/gas mark 7. Grease and line 2 baking sheets with nonstick baking parchment.

Melt the butter and syrup slowly in a medium-sized pan over a low heat.

Meanwhile, peel and coarsely grate the carrots and add to the butter and syrup with the orange zest. Stir to combine and leave over a low heat for 2 minutes. Sift the flour into a large bowl, then add the bran and sugar and fully incorporate (I find that using my hands is the most efficient way). Carefully pour the carrot and butter mixture into the dry ingredients and quickly combine to form a firm, smooth dough, using a wooden spoon. Roll the dough into large walnut-sized balls and flatten with dampened fingers into 5 mm/¼ in thick discs. Bake for 10–12 minutes or the cookies are golden brown. Leave to cool on the baking sheets for 2 minutes before transferring to a wire rack to cool completely. Once cooled, scatter over the candied peel to decorate.

Blueberry Cookies

Preparation time: 20 minutes
Cooking time: 12 minutes
Makes 30–35

120 g/4 oz/1 cup fresh blueberries
100 g/3½ oz/⅓ cup golden granulated sugar
120 g/4 oz/1 cup plain (all-purpose) flour
60 g/2 oz/½ cup rolled oats
60 g/2 oz/½ cup unsalted butter, plus extra for greasing
1 tablespoon golden syrup
3 tablespoons low fat natural yogurt

To decorate
30 g/1 oz/¼ cup dried blueberries

Dried blueberries are becoming more and more readily available, but if you are unable to find them simply reserve some of the whole fresh ones to use for decoration.

Preheat the oven to 200°C/400°F/gas mark 6. Grease and line 2 baking sheets with a little butter and nonstick baking parchment.

Mash the blueberries with a fork until broken down but not puréed and set aside. Mix the sugar, flour and oats together. Melt the butter and syrup in a small pan over a low heat, then pour over the dry ingredients and stir quickly until the mixture resembles lumpy breadcrumbs.
Add the yogurt 1 tablespoon at a time until you have a sticky dough. Drop teaspoons of the dough on to the baking sheets, leaving a 5 cm/2 in space between each one, as they will spread when baking, and flatten with dampened fingers into 5 cm/2 in diameter discs.

To decorate, sprinkle over the dried blueberries, pressing them down slightly. Bake for 12 minutes until the edges of the cookies begin to brown slightly. Leave to cool on the baking sheets for 4 minutes before transferring to a wire rack to cool completely.

Pecan Crunch Cookies

Preparation time: 20 minutes
Cooking time: 10–12 minutes
Makes 20–24

100 g/3½ oz/1 cup roughly chopped pecan nuts
120 g/4 oz/1 cup plain (all-purpose) flour
1/4 teaspoon baking powder
60 g/2 oz/½ cup rolled oats
120 g/4 oz/½ cup golden caster (superfine) sugar
60 g/2 oz/½ cup unsalted butter, softened
1 tablespoon golden syrup
3 tablespoons low fat natural (plain) yogurt

To decorate
20–24 pecan nuts

Research has shown that eating a handful of pecan nuts every day reduces cholesterol levels and could possibly be used as an alternative to cholesterol-reducing drugs.

Preheat the oven to 150°C/300°F/gas mark 2. Grease and line 2 baking sheets with nonstick baking parchment.

Put the chopped pecans in a large bowl. Sift the flour and baking powder on to the nuts. Add the oats and sugar and stir to combine. Melt the butter and syrup in a pan over a medium heat. Pour over the dry ingredients and stir quickly until the mixture resembles lumpy breadcrumbs, then gradually add the yogurt. Gather the mixture together into a ball – it should be a fairly solid dough. Roll the dough into golfball-sized balls, place on the baking sheets and flatten with dampened fingers into 5 mm/¼ in thick discs. Place a pecan nut in the centre of each cookie. Bake for 10–12 minutes or until the cookies have turned golden brown. Leave to cool on the baking sheets for 2 minutes before transferring to a wire rack to cool completely.

Coconut and Lime Cookies

Preparation time: 10–15 minutes
Cooking time: 10–12 minutes
Makes 16

120 g/4 oz/1 cup plain (all-purpose) flour
150 g/5 oz/2 cups desiccated coconut
120 g/4 oz/½ cup caster (superfine) sugar
½ teaspoon baking powder
finely grated zest of 2 limes
60 g/2 oz/½ cup unsalted butter
5 tablespoons low fat natural (plain) yogurt
2–3 tablespoons semi-skimmed (half fat) milk

To decorate
2 tablespoons desiccated coconut
finely grated zest of 1 lime

The flavours of this cookie are inspired by classic Jamaican ingredients. The marriage of the succulent coconut with the fragrant lime is a delicious combination. The decoration is purely optional, as the cookies look simple but elegant without.

Preheat the oven to 200°C/400°F/gas mark 6. Grease and line 2 baking sheets with nonstick baking parchment.

Stir the flour, coconut, sugar, baking powder and lime zest together, making sure that the lime zest is evenly dispersed. Melt the butter in a small pan, then leave to cool for 1–2 minutes before pouring into the dry ingredients. Mix in the butter using a wooden spoon and gradually add the yogurt. Stir in the milk, 1 tablespoon at a time. Gather the mixture together into a ball and knead for 30 seconds until you have a smooth dough. Roll the dough into balls with hands dusted with flour to prevent them sticking. Place on the baking sheets and flatten into discs. Bake for 10–12 minutes or until the cookies have a slight golden tinge around the edges. Transfer to a wire rack to cool completely.

To decorate, mix the coconut and lime zest together and sprinkle over the cooled cookies.

Apple and Oat Cookies

Preparation time: 15 minutes
Cooking time: 10–12 minutes
Makes 35–40

375 g/12 oz/3 cups rolled oats
120 g/4 oz/1 cup plain (all-purpose) flour
½ teaspoon bicarbonate of soda (baking soda)
pinch of fine salt
60 g/2 oz/½ cup unsalted butter
240 g/8 oz/1 cup apple sauce
250 ml/8 fl oz/1 cup buttermilk or plain yogurt

To decorate
3 tablespoons caster (superfine) sugar
1 teaspoon ground ginger

I like to make the full amount but only bake half. I form the other half into discs, stack them between layers of nonstick baking parchment and freeze in a freezerproof box. (Baking from frozen, you may need to increase the baking time by 2–3 minutes.)

Preheat the oven to 200°C/400°F/gas mark 6. Grease and line 2 baking sheets with nonstick baking parchment.

Mix the oats, flour, bicarbonate of soda and salt together in a food processor. Place the butter in a small pan and heat until just melted. With the motor of the food processor running, pour the butter into the dry ingredients until completely absorbed. Add the apple sauce and pulse to incorporate. Gradually add the buttermilk or yogurt until you have a sticky dough. Mix the sugar and ground ginger together and place on a shallow plate. Take scant teaspoons of the sticky dough and roll in the sugar and ginger mixture. Place on the baking sheets, flattening slightly with dampened fingers into 5mm/¼ in thick discs. Bake for 10–12 minutes or until the cookies are just starting to colour around the edges. Leave to cool on the baking sheets for 2 minutes before transferring to a wire rack. Serve at room temperature.

Date and Walnut Cookies

Preparation time: 20–25 minutes
Cooking time: 12–14 minutes
Makes 16–18

120 g/4 oz/1 cup plain (all-purpose) flour, sifted
120 g/4 oz/1 cup rolled oats
½ teaspoon baking powder
120 g/4 oz/½ cup caster (superfine) sugar
60 g/2 oz/½ cup walnuts
120 g/4 oz/1 cup stoneless dates
60 g/2 oz/½ cup unsalted butter
5–6 tablespoons semi-skimmed (half fat) milk

To decorate
16–18 walnut halves

If you prefer fewer chunks in your cookies, you can tip the walnuts and dates into a food processor and blitz until fine.

Preheat the oven to 200°C/400°F/gas mark 6. Grease and line 2 baking sheets with nonstick baking parchment.

Mix the flour, oats, baking powder and sugar together. Roughly chop the walnuts and dates and stir into the dry ingredients. Place the butter in a small pan and heat until just melted. Pour into the dry ingredients and stir with a wooden spoon until the mixture resembles chunky breadcrumbs. Add the milk, 1 tablespoon at a time, until you can just gather the mixture into a sticky ball of dough.

Roll the dough into balls, place well apart on the baking sheets and flatten with dampened fingers into 5 mm/¼ in thick discs. Place a walnut half in the centre of each cookie. Bake for 12–14 minutes. Transfer to a wire rack to cool.

Almond and Cinnamon Cookies

Preparation time: 10 minutes
Cooking time: 10–12 minutes
Makes 24

120 g/4 oz/1 cup unsalted butter, softened
100 g/3 ½ oz/⅓ cup brown sugar
2 egg whites, at room temperature
120 g/4 oz/1 cup plain (all-purpose) flour
2 teaspoons ground cinnamon
60 g/2 oz/½ cup rolled oats
4 tablespoons natural bran
150 g/5 oz/1 cup blanched almonds

To decorate
60 g/2 oz/¾ cup dark chocolate
24 whole blanched almonds

Preheat the oven to 160°C/325°F/gas mark 3. Grease and line 2 baking sheets with nonstick baking parchment.

Place the butter and sugar in a food processor and cream until slightly paler and fluffy before adding the egg whites one at a time. Sift the flour and tip into the food processor with the cinnamon, oats and bran. Pulse 4 or 5 times until you have a ball of dough. Roughly chop the almonds, remove the dough from the food processor and knead in the almonds with lightly floured hands. Roll the dough into golfball-sized balls, place on the baking sheets and flatten slightly with dampened fingers. Bake for 10–12 minutes or until the cookies turn golden. Leave to cool for 1–2 minutes before transferring to a wire rack to cool completely.

To decorate, break up the chocolate into pieces and place in a heatproof glass bowl over a pan of simmering water, making sure that the bowl does not touch the water as it could burn the chocolate. Once melted, remove the bowl from the pan and set aside for 2 minutes to cool slightly. Tip in the almonds and stir until they are evenly coated in chocolate. Using a teaspoon, place an almond on the centre of each cookie with a little extra chocolate, creating a little pool of chocolate around each nut. Once set, the cookies are ready to eat.

Cranberry and Orange Cookies

Preparation time: 15 minutes
Cooking time: 8–10 minutes
Makes 24

120 g/4 oz/1 cup unsalted butter, softened
120 g/4 oz/1 cup caster (superfine) sugar
2 eggs, at room temperature
240 g/8 oz/2 cups plain (all-purpose) flour
1 teaspoon baking powder
½ teaspoon fine salt
100 g/3½ oz/1 cup sliced dried cranberries
2 tablespoons finely grated orange zest

To decorate
60 g/2 oz/½ cup sliced dried cranberries.

Dried cranberries have traditionally been seen as a classic Thanksgiving/Christmas dinner acompaniment. However, cranberries, especially dried cranberries, are now available all year round so you can make these cookies whenever the mood takes you.

Preheat the oven to 160°C/325°F/gas mark 3. Grease and line 2 baking sheets with nonstick baking parchment.

Cream the butter and sugar together using a wooden spoon or electric hand whisk. Add the eggs, one at a time, only adding the second one when the first is fully incorporated. Beat until smooth – if the mixture curdles slightly, don't worry, just beat in 1 tablespoon of the flour. Sift the flour, baking powder and salt together and stir into the mixture. Roughly chop the cranberries and stir in with the orange zest. Spoon heaped tablespoons of the dough on to the baking sheets, leaving a 5 cm/2 in space between each one, as they will spread when baking, and flatten with dampened fingers into 5 mm/¼ in thick discs. Decorate each cookie with 3 or 4 of the dried cranberries and bake for 8–10 minutes. Leave to cool for 2–3 minutes on the baking sheets before transferring to a wire rack to cool completely. Serve at room temperature.

Three-Seed Cookies

Preparation time: 10 minutes
Cooking time: 10 minutes
Makes 24

120g/4 oz/1 cup unsalted butter, softened
100g/3½ oz/⅓ cup brown sugar
2 tablespoons runny honey
2 egg whites, at room temperature
120 g/4 oz/1 cup plain (all-purpose) flour
60 g/2 oz/½ cup rolled oats
4 tablespoons natural bran
60 g/2 oz/½ cup sesame seeds
60 g/2 oz/½ cup sunflower seeds
60 g/2 oz/½ cup pumpkin seeds

To decorate
1 tablespoon sesame seeds
1 tablespoon sunflower seeds
1 tablespoon pumpkin seeds

Preheat the oven to 160°C/325°F/gas mark 3. Grease and line 2 baking sheets with nonstick baking parchment.

Place the butter, sugar and honey in a food processor and blend for 2–3 minutes until the colour of the mixture lightens slightly (you may need to stop and scrape down the sides every so often). Add the egg whites one at a time, blending for a few seconds between each addition. Add the flour, oats and bran and pulse until just combined – you don't want to overmix because the flour will become tough. Add the seeds and pulse once or twice before carefully removing the dough from the machine and working the seeds in with your hands. Roll the dough into golfball-sized balls, place on the baking sheets and flatten with dampened fingers into 5 mm/¼ in thick discs.

To decorate, mix together the three types of seeds and scatter over the cookies. Bake for 10 minutes. Leave to cool on the baking sheets for 2–3 minutes before transferring to a wire rack to cool.

Oat and Sultana Cookies

Preparation time: 15–20 minutes
Cooking time: 10–12 minutes
Makes 10

120 g/4 oz/1 cup plain (all-purpose) flour
60 g/2 oz/½ cup rolled oats
40 g/1½ oz/½ cup desiccated coconut
½ teaspoon baking powder
120g/4 oz/½ cup caster (superfine) sugar
50 g/2 oz/½ cup unsalted butter
1 tablespoon golden syrup
75 g/3 oz/½ cup sultanas
3–4 tablespoons low fat natural (plain) yogurt

These delicious, healthy cookies have a chewy centre and the butter is absorbed by the sultanas, which plump up and become the decoration of the cookies.

Preheat the oven to 200°C/400°F/gas mark 6. Grease and line a large baking sheet with nonstick baking parchment.

Mix the flour, oats, coconut, baking powder and sugar together. Place the butter, syrup and sultanas in a small pan and melt slowly. Pour into the dry ingredients and mix to incorporate, creating lumpy breadcrumbs. Gradually add the yogurt, 1 tablespoon at a time, until you have a soft dough. Roll the dough into golfball-sized balls, place on the baking sheets and flatten with dampened fingers into 5 mm/¼ in thick discs. Bake for 10–12 minutes. Transfer to a wire rack to cool completely. If they are not to be eaten immediately, the cookies should be cooled completely before being stored in an airtight container.

with family
& friends

Christmas Tree Decorations

Preparation time: 40 minutes
Cooking time: 6–8 minutes
Makes 30

90 g/3 oz/¾ cup unsalted butter, softened
90 g/3 oz/¾ cup caster (superfine) sugar
1 medium egg, at room temperature
½ teaspoon vanilla extract
240 g/8 oz/2 cups plain (all-purpose) flour, plus extra
   for dusting
1 teaspoon mixed spice

To decorate
2–3 tablespoons icing (confectioners') sugar
120 g/4 oz/½ cup white regal icing
120 g/4 oz/½ cup red regal icing
120 g/4 oz/½ cup green regal icing
60 g/2 oz/½ cup brown regal icing
2–3 tablespoons apricot jam, sieved
edible silver balls
edible glitter

You can make any combination of Christmas shapes, and the colours I have given are only a guideline – use whichever you like best.

Preheat the oven to 180°C/350°F/gas mark 4. Grease and line 2–3 baking sheets with nonstick baking parchment.

Cream the butter and sugar together until pale and fluffy using a wooden spoon or electric hand whisk. Add the egg and vanilla extract and beat well – don't worry if the mixture curdles slightly, just beat in 1 tablespoon of the flour. Sift the flour and mixed spice together and fold into the mixture until you have a stiff dough. If the dough seems too soft to roll out, refrigerate for 20 minutes.

Roll out the dough on a lightly floured cool surface or between 2 sheets of clingfilm until 2.5 mm/⅛ in thick. Using Christmas cookie cutters such as hearts, Father Christmas, stockings, stars, trees, reindeer, snowmen and snowflakes dusted with a little flour, cut out as many shapes as possible, as the more you have to reroll the dough, the tougher it will become. Using a metal palette knife or fish slice, carefully lift out the Christmas shapes and place on the baking sheets. Bake for 6–8 minutes or until the cookies start to turn a very pale golden colour. As soon as they come out of the oven, make a hole in the top of each cookie with a metal skewer. Transfer to a wire rack and leave to cool.

Once cool, you can decorate the cookies. Roll out the white regal icing first, on a cool surface dusted with a little icing sugar or between 2 sheets of clingfilm until 2.5 mm/⅛ in thick. Using the same Christmas cutters as before, dusted this time with a little icing sugar, cut out about 7 shapes. Repeat this method with the red, green and brown icing until you have enough for all the cookies.

Using a clean paintbrush, paint a little of the sieved jam on each cookie to ensure that the icing will stick, place the icing shapes on the cookies and press down lightly. Push the skewer through the holes again to make holes in the icing as well as the cookies. Decorate each cookie with the silver balls, pushing them down right into the icing to secure. Brush the snowflakes with a little of the sieved jam and sprinkle over the edible glitter, shaking off any excess. Thread some fine ribbon or coloured string through the holes. The decorations are now ready to hang on your tree.

Christmas Stockings

Preparation time: 30–35 minutes
Cooking time: 7–8 minutes
Makes 24

90 g/3 oz/¾ cup unsalted butter, softened
90 g/3 oz/¾ cup caster (superfine) sugar
1 medium egg, at room temperature
½ teaspoon vanilla extract
240 g/8 oz/2 cups plain (all purpose) flour, plus extra
   for dusting
1 teaspoon mixed spice

To decorate
2–3 tablespoons icing (confectioner's) sugar
360 g/12 oz/1½ cups red regal icing
2–3 tablespoons marmalade, sieved
30 g/1 oz/¼ cup pale white regal icing
edible silver balls

These cookies are a fun idea for children to help to make as Christmas gifts – homemade presents have a special charm.

Preheat the oven to 180°C/350°F/gas mark 4. Grease and line 2 baking sheets with nonstick baking parchment.

Cream the butter and sugar together until pale and fluffy using a wooden spoon or electric hand whisk. Add the egg and vanilla extract and beat well – don't worry if the mixture curdles slightly, just beat in 1 tablespoon of the flour. Sift the flour and mixed spice together and fold into the mixture until you have a stiff dough. If the dough seems too soft to roll out, refrigerate for 20 minutes.

Roll out the dough on a lightly floured cool surface or between 2 sheets of clingfilm until 2.5 mm/⅛ in thick. Using a Christmas stocking-shaped cookie cutter dusted with a little flour, or the stencil on page 93, cut out as many stockings as possible, as the more you have to reroll the dough, the tougher it will become. Using a metal palette knife or fish slice, carefully lift out the stocking shapes and place on the baking sheets. Bake for 7–8 minutes or until the cookies start to turn a very pale golden colour. Transfer to a wire rack and leave to cool.

Once cool, you can decorate the cookies. Roll out the red regal icing on a cool surface dusted with a little icing sugar or between 2 sheets of clingfilm until 2.5 mm/⅛ in thick. Using the same cutter as before, dusted this time with a little icing sugar, cut out the same number of stocking shapes. Trim off the top rectangular part of the stocking and, using a clean paintbrush, paint a little of the sieved marmalade on each cookie to ensure that the icing will stick, place the icing shapes on the cookies and press down lightly. Roll out the white regal icing to the same thickness as the red and, using just the top part of the cutter around the edge of the icing, cut out the stocking tops – you may need to trim the edges with a knife. Place one on each cookie. Finally, decorate the white part of the icing with a row of silver balls and push them down right into the icing to secure.

3D Christmas Tree

Preparation time: 30 minutes
Cooking time: 6–8 minutes
Chilling time: 20 minutes
Makes 1 big tree

90 g/3 oz/¾ cup unsalted butter, softened
90 g/3 oz/¾ cup caster (superfine) sugar
1 medium egg, at room temperature
½ teaspoon vanilla extract
240 g/8 oz/2 cups plain (all-purpose) flour, plus extra
    for dusting
1 teaspoon ground cinnamon

To decorate
60 g/2 oz/½ cup white regal icing
1 small tube of white writing icing
12 edible silver balls

This cookie is a little different, as it can be used as a
table decoration or a general Christmas decoration.
You can enjoy looking at it and then later everyone
can break off a piece and enjoy eating it. Any leftover
scraps of dough can be rerolled and used to make
other Christmas cookies.

Preheat the oven to 180°C/350°F/gas mark 4. Grease and
line a large baking sheet with nonstick baking parchment.

Cream the butter and sugar until pale and fluffy using a
wooden spoon or electric hand whisk. Add the egg and
vanilla extract and beat well – don't worry if the mixture
curdles slightly, just beat in 1 tablespoon of the flour. Sift the
flour and cinnamon together and fold into the mixture until
you have a stiff dough. If the dough seems too soft to roll
out, refrigerate for 20 minutes.

Roll out the dough on a lightly floured cool surface or
between 2 sheets of clingfilm until 2.5 mm/⅛ in thick.
Using a Christmas tree-shaped cookie cutter dusted with a
little flour, or the stencil on page 92, cut out 2 large trees.
Using 2 fish slices, carefully lift out the trees and place on
the baking sheet. Cut one of the trees in half from top to
bottom. Bake for 6–8 minutes or until the cookies start to
turn a very pale golden colour. As soon they come out of the
oven, recut the tree you cut before. Leave on the baking sheet
to cool for 2 minutes before transferring to a wire rack to
cool completely.

Once cool, you can decorate the cookies. Remove a small
piece of the white regal icing, roll out until 2.5 mm/⅛ in
thick and cut out a small star that will sit on top of the tree.
Roll the remaining white regal icing into a ball, flatten
slightly in dampened hands and place in the centre of your
chosen serving plate. This will be the base for your tree to
stand in. Pipe a thin line of white writing icing along each
cut edge of the half trees, stick one half to one side of the
whole tree and the other on the other side and hold them in
place for 2–3 minutes while the icing dries. Push the trunk
of the tree into the icing stand until it feels secure. Then pipe
along where the two trees are attached to hide any excess
icing that may have oozed out. Pipe a little star on the tip of
each branch, then stick a silver ball on each star. Pipe a
further star on the top of the tree, which will help to secure
the cut-out star. Stick the cut-out star on the top of the tree
and your tree is finished.

Christmas Cake Cookies

Preparation time: 25 minutes
Cooking time: 10–12 minutes
Makes 24

90 g/3 oz/¾ cup unsalted butter, softened
90 g/3 oz/¾ cup caster (superfine) sugar
1 medium egg, at room temperature
½ teaspoon vanilla extract
2 tablespoon dark rum
90 g/3 oz/½ cup candied peel, chopped
45 g/1½ oz/¼ cup glacé cherries, roughly chopped
3 tablespoons roughly chopped stem ginger
½ teaspoon mixed spice
½ teaspoon ground cinnamon
½ teaspoon ground cloves
½ teaspoon ground ginger
240 g/8 oz/2 cups plain (all-purpose) flour, plus extra
   for dusting

To decorate
12 glacé cherries, halved

These cookies are a lovely way of enjoying all the flavours of a Christmas cake in no time at all.

Preheat the oven to 180°C/350°F/gas mark 4. Grease and line 2–3 baking sheets with nonstick baking parchment.

Cream the butter and sugar together until pale and fluffy using a wooden spoon or electric hand whisk. Add the egg, then stir in the vanilla essence, rum, candied peel, cherries and stem ginger and beat well. Sift the spices with the flour and fold into the mixture until you have a soft dough. Roll the dough into golfball-sized balls, place on the baking sheets and flatten with dampened fingers into 5mm/¼ in thick discs. Place half a cherry in the centre of each cookie. Bake for 10–12 minutes. Transfer to a wire rack and leave to cool.

Angel Cookies

Preparation time: 40 minutes
Cooking time: 7–8 minutes
Makes 24

90 g/3 oz/¾ cup unsalted butter, softened
90 g/3 oz/¾ cup caster (superfine) sugar
1 medium egg, at room temperature
½ teaspoon almond extract
240 g/8 oz/2 cups plain (all-purpose) flour, plus extra
   for dusting

To decorate
2–3 tablespoons icing (confectioners') sugar
360 g/12 oz/1½ cups white regal icing
2–3 tablespoons apricot jam, sieved
edible glitter or dust

Preheat the oven to 180°C/350°F/gas mark 4. Grease and line 2 baking sheets with nonstick baking parchment.

Cream the butter and sugar together until pale and fluffy. Add the egg and almond extract and beat well – don't worry if the mixture curdles slightly, just beat in 1 tablespoon of the flour. Sift the flour and fold into the mixture until you have a stiff dough. If the dough seems too soft to roll, refrigerate for 20 minutes.

Roll out the dough on a lightly floured surface until 5 mm /¼ in thick. Using an angel-shaped cookie cutter dusted with a little flour, cut out as many angels as possible, as the more you have to reroll the dough, the tougher it will become. Using a metal palette knife, carefully lift out the angels on to the baking sheets. Bake for 7–8 minutes or until the cookies turn golden in colour. Transfer to a wire rack and leave to cool.

To decorate, roll out the regal icing on a cool surface dusted with a little icing sugar until 2.5 mm/⅛ in thick. Using the same cutter as before, dusted this time with a little icing sugar, cut out the same number of angel shapes. Stick the icing shapes on to the cookies using a little jam and press down lightly. Brush a thin layer of jam on top of the icing, sprinkle over the edible glitter or dust, and shake off any excess before serving.

Snowmen Cookies

Preparation time: 40 minutes
Cooking time: 7–8 minutes
Makes 24

90 g/3 oz/¾ cup unsalted butter, softened
90 g/3 oz/¾ cup caster (superfine) sugar
1 medium egg, at room temperature
½ teaspoon almond essence
240 g/8 oz/2 cups plain (all-purpose) flour, plus extra
    for dusting

To decorate
2–3 tablespoons icing (confectioners') sugar
360 g/12 oz/1½ cups white regal icing
2–3 tablespoons apricot jam, sieved
1 small tube of black writing icing
half a carrot
ribbon

You can the make the scarves out of any ribbon. I find it's an excellent way of using up the cut-offs left over from wrapping my Christmas presents.

Preheat the oven to 180°C/350°F/gas mark 4. Grease and line 2 baking sheets with nonstick baking parchment.

Cream the butter and sugar together until pale and fluffy using a wooden spoon or electric hand whisk. Add the egg and almond essence and beat well – don't worry if the mixture curdles slightly, just beat in 1 tablespoon of the flour. Sift the flour and fold into the mixture until you have a stiff dough. If the dough seems too soft to roll out, refrigerate for 20 minutes.

Roll out the dough on a lightly floured cool surface or between 2 sheets of clingfilm until 2.5 mm/⅛ in thick. Using a snowman-shaped cookie cutter dusted with a little flour, or the stencil on page 93, cut out as many snowmen as possible, as the more you have to reroll the dough, the tougher it will become. Using a metal palette knife or fish slice, carefully lift out the snowmen and place on the baking sheets. Bake for 7–8 minutes or until the snowmen start to turn a very pale golden colour. Transfer to a wire rack and leave to cool.

Once cool, you can decorate the cookies. Roll out the white regal icing on a cool surface dusted with a little icing sugar or between 2 sheets of clingfilm until 2.5 mm/⅛ in thick. Using the same snowman cutter, dusted this time with a little icing sugar, cut out the same number of snowmen shapes. Using a clean paintbrush, paint a little of the sieved jam on each cookie to ensure that the icing will stick, place the icing shapes on the cookies and press down lightly. Using the black writing icing, pipe on eyes and buttons. Peel and finely slice the carrot and from the slices carefully cut out little noses. Stick the carrot noses into the icing and tie a little piece of ribbon around the snowmen's necks as scarves.

Heart Cookies

Preparation time: 40 minutes
Cooking time: 3–8 minutes
Chilling time: 20 minutes
Makes 1 complete stack plus a few extra small ones

90 g/3 oz/¾ cup unsalted butter, softened
90 g/3 oz/¾ cup caster (superfine) sugar
1 medium egg, at room temperature
½ teaspoon vanilla extract
240 g/8 oz/2 cups plain (all-purpose) flour, plus extra
    for dusting

To decorate
2–3 tablespoons icing (confectioners') sugar
30 g/1 oz/¼ cup white regal icing
2–3 tablespoons apricot jam, sieved
1 small tube of white writing icing
10 edible silver balls
edible pink dust
20 pink candy balls

This is the perfect pretty gift to give to someone
who you love. You could present it in a box with some
pale pink tissue paper scrunched up in the base or
wrap it in a sheet of cellophane gathered and tied
with pink ribbon.

Preheat the oven to 180°C/350°F/gas mark 4. Grease and
line 2–3 baking sheets with nonstick baking parchment.

Cream the butter and sugar together until pale and fluffy
using a wooden spoon or electric hand whisk. Add the egg
and vanilla extract and beat well – don't worry if the mixture
curdles slightly, just beat in 1 tablespoon of the flour. Sift
the flour and fold into the mixture until you have a stiff
dough. If the dough seems too soft to roll out, refrigerate
for 20 minutes.

Roll out the dough on a lightly floured cool surface or
between 2 sheets of clingfilm until 2.5 mm/⅛ in thick.
Using either 6 heart-shaped cutters in different sizes dusted
with a little flour, or the stencils on page 88, cut out a full set
of hearts; you may have enough dough to make some extra
small hearts as well. Using a metal palette knife or fish slice,
carefully lift out the heart shapes and place on the baking
sheets. Bake for 3–8 minutes. You will need to take out the
smallest heart after 3 minutes, then keep taking out each
heart in order of size every minute until you remove the
largest heart. Transfer to a wire rack to cool completely.

Once cool, you can decorate the cookies. Start with the
largest and work your way up to the smallest. Using a small
star piping nozzle, pipe stars all round the edge of the largest
heart then set aside to set. The next size up cookie should be
left plain. For the third biggest cookie roll out the white regal
icing between 2 sheets of clingfilm until 2.5 mm/⅛ in thick.
Using the same cutter as before, dusted this time with a little
icing sugar, cut out a heart shape, brush with a little of the
sieved jam, place the icing shape on the cookie, press down
lightly and decorate with silver balls, pressing them down to
secure. The next size up cookie should be left plain. Paint
the second smallest heart with a little of the sieved jam and
sprinkle with the pink dust, shaking off any excess. Spread
the smallest heart with a little of the white writing icing and
carefully place the pink candy balls round the edge. Set aside
to harden for a few minutes before stacking up the hearts in
order of size.

Slimey Green Ghost Cookies

Preparation time: 30 minutes
Cooking time: 7–8 minutes
Makes 24

90 g/3 oz/¾ cup unsalted butter, softened
90 g/3 oz/¾ cup caster (superfine) sugar
1 medium egg, at room temperature
½ teaspoon vanilla extract
2 teaspoons finely grated lime zest
240 g/8 oz/2 cups plain (all-purpose) flour, plus extra
    for dusting

To decorate
48 large green jelly candies

If you can't find a ghost-shaped cookie cutter, you can design your own simple ghost-like shape and cut it out with a small knife. When the cookies are decorated with the green slime, they become chewy on top with a crunchy base.

Preheat the oven to 180°C/350°F/gas mark 4. Grease and line 2 baking sheets with nonstick baking parchment.

Cream the butter and sugar together until pale and fluffy using a wooden spoon or electric hand whisk. Add the egg and vanilla extract and beat well – don't worry if the mixture curdles slightly, just beat in 1 tablespoon of the flour. Sift the flour and fold into the mixture until you have a stiff dough. If the dough seems too soft to roll out, refrigerate for 20 minutes.

Roll out the dough on a lightly floured cool surface or between 2 sheets of clingfilm until 2.5 mm/⅛ in thick. Using a ghost-shaped cookie cutter dusted with a little flour, cut out as many ghosts as possible, as the more you have to reroll the dough, the tougher it will become. Using a metal palette knife or fish slice, carefully lift out the ghosts and place on the baking sheets. Bake for 7–8 minutes or until the cookies start to turn a very pale golden colour. Transfer to a wire rack and leave to cool.

Once cool, you can decorate the cookies. Melt the jelly candies in a small pan over a low to medium heat for 3–5 minutes. As soon as the jellies have melted, remove from the heat and very carefully, as the mixture will be very hot, spoon the green slime over the cookies. Leave on the wire rack to cool completely and set.

Bat Cookies

Preparation time: 35–40 minutes
Chilling time: 1 hour
Cooking time: 5–6 minutes
Makes 30–35

60 g/2 oz/½ cup unsalted butter, softened
240 g/8 oz/2 cups plain (all-purpose) flour
90 g/3 oz/½ cup brown sugar
3–4 tablespoons black treacle
1 medium egg, at room temperature, lightly beaten
    (you will only need to use half)
½ tablespoon finely grated orange zest
½ teaspoon mixed spice
½ teaspoon ground ginger
¼ teaspoon bicarbonate of soda (baking soda)
pinch of fine salt
extra flour for rolling

To decorate
2 tablespoons icing (confectioners') sugar
260 g/12 oz/1½ cups black regal icing
2 tablespoons marmalade, sieved
1 small tube of bright green writing icing

These cookies may look similar to the cat cookies (see opposite), with their black and green decoration, but the black treacle makes them darker and the spices give them an extra kick. Little boys who deem angels, butterflies and hearts too girly may think these manly enough to make.

Preheat the oven to 190°C/375°F/gas mark 5. Grease and line 2 baking sheets with nonstick baking parchment.

Cream the butter until smooth. Add half of the flour, the sugar, treacle, half of the egg, orange zest, spices, bicarbonate of soda and salt. Beat until smooth with a wooden spoon or electric hand whisk. Stir in the remaining flour and knead for 30 seconds until you have a smooth dough. Wrap the dough in clingfilm and chill for 1 hour.

Roll out the dough on a lightly floured cool surface or between 2 sheets of clingfilm until 5 mm/¼ in thick. Using a bat-shaped cookie cutter, cut out 30–35 bats. Using a metal palette knife or fish slice, carefully lift out the bats and place on the baking sheets, leaving a 2.5 cm/1 in space between each, as they will spread when baking. Bake for 5–6 minutes. Leave to cool on the baking sheets for 2 minutes before transferring to a wire rack to cool completely.

Once cool, you can decorate the cookies. Roll out the black regal icing on a cool surface dusted with a little icing sugar or between 2 sheets of clingfilm until 2.5 mm/⅛ in thick. Using the same cutter as before, dusted this time with a little icing sugar, cut out the same number of bat shapes. Using a clean paintbrush, paint a little of the sieved marmalade on each cookie to ensure that the icing will stick, place the icing shapes on the cookies and press down lightly. Using the bright green writing icing, draw 2 dots on each bat for eyes.

Cat Cookies

Preparation time: 25–30 minutes
Cooking time: 7–8 minutes
Makes 24

90 g/3 oz/¾ cup unsalted butter, softened
90 g/3 oz/¾ cup caster (superfine) sugar
1 medium egg, at room temperature
½ teaspoon vanilla extract
240 g/8 oz/2 cups plain (all-purpose) flour, plus extra
    for dusting

To decorate
2–3 tablespoons icing (confectioners') sugar
360 g/12 oz/1½ cups black regal icing
2–3 tablespoons apricot jam, sieved
1 small tube of bright green writing icing

Preheat the oven to 180°C/350°F/gas mark 4. Grease and line 2 baking sheets with nonstick baking parchment.

Cream the butter and sugar together until pale and fluffy using a wooden spoon or electric hand whisk. Add the egg and vanilla extract and beat well – don't worry if the mixture curdles slightly, just beat in 1 tablespoon of the flour. Sift the flour and mixed spice together and fold into the mixture until you have a stiff dough. If the dough seems too soft to roll out, refrigerate for 20 minutes.

Roll out the dough on a lightly floured cool surface or between 2 sheets of clingfilm until 2.5 mm/⅛ in thick. Using a cat-shaped cookie cutter dusted with a little flour, or the stencil on page 89, cut out as many cats as possible, as the more you have to reroll the dough, the tougher it will become. Using a metal palette knife or fish slice, carefully lift out the cats and place on the baking sheets. Bake for 7–8 minutes or until the cookies start to turn a very pale golden colour. Transfer to a wire rack and leave to cool.

Once cool, you can decorate the cookies. Roll out the black regal icing on a cool surface dusted with a little icing sugar or between 2 sheets of clingfilm until 2.5 mm/⅛ in thick. Using the same cutter as before, dusted this time with a little icing sugar, cut out the same number of cat shapes. Using a clean paintbrush, paint a little of the sieved jam on each cookie to ensure that the icing will stick, place the icing shapes on the cookies and press down lightly. Using the green writing icing, draw 2 dots on each cat for eyes.

Scrabble Cookies

Preparation time: 35 minutes
Cooking time: 5 minutes
Chilling time: 20 minutes
Makes 30

90 g/3 oz/¾ cup unsalted butter, softened
90 g/3 oz/¾ cup caster (superfine) sugar
1 medium egg, at room temperature
½ teaspoon vanilla extract
240 g/8 oz/2 cups plain (all-purpose) flour, plus extra
    for dusting

To decorate
2–3 tablespoons icing (confectioners') sugar
360 g/12 oz/1½ cups white regal icing
2–3 tablespoons apricot jam, sieved
1 small tube of coloured writing icing

For this gift idea you could write any words you like, from someone's name to 'Happy Birthday', 'Be My Valentine', 'I Love You', 'Good Luck' or 'Congratulations'. You could jumble the letters up and present them in a pretty gift box lined with tissue paper. Your lucky recipient can then move the letters around to work out your message to them. So much more romantic than a text (SMS) message.

Preheat the oven to 180°C/350°F/gas mark 4. Grease and line 2 baking sheets with nonstick baking parchment.

Cream the butter and sugar together until pale and fluffy using a wooden spoon or electric hand whisk. Add the egg and vanilla extract and beat well – don't worry if the mixture curdles slightly, just beat in 1 tablespoon of the flour. Sift the flour and fold into the mixture until you have a stiff dough. If the dough seems too soft to roll out, refrigerate for 20 minutes.

Roll out the dough on a lightly floured cool surface or between 2 sheets of clingfilm until 2.5 mm/⅛ in thick. Using a 4–5 cm/1½ –2 in diameter cookie cutter dusted with a little flour, cut out as many circles as possible, as the more you have to reroll the dough, the tougher it will become. Using a metal palette knife or fish slice, carefully lift out the circles and place on the baking sheets. Bake for 5 minutes or until the cookies start to turn a very pale golden colour. Transfer to a wire rack and leave to cool.

Once cool, you can decorate the cookies. Roll out the white regal icing on a cool surface dusted with a little icing sugar or between 2 sheets of clingfilm until 2.5 mm/⅛ in thick. Using the same cutter as before, dusted this time with a little icing sugar, cut out the same number of circles. Using a clean paintbrush, paint a little of the sieved jam on each cookie to ensure that the icing will stick, place the icing shapes on the cookies and press down lightly. Using the coloured writing icing, write a letter on each cookie to spell out the name or message.

How to use the stencils

It is not essential to have a large collection of cookie cutters because making your own templates is easy.

Take a sheet of tracing paper and place over the chosen stencil. Trace the shape using a pencil, carefully cut out the shape with scissors, place the shape on the rolled-out dough and cut around the shape using a small knife.

stencils

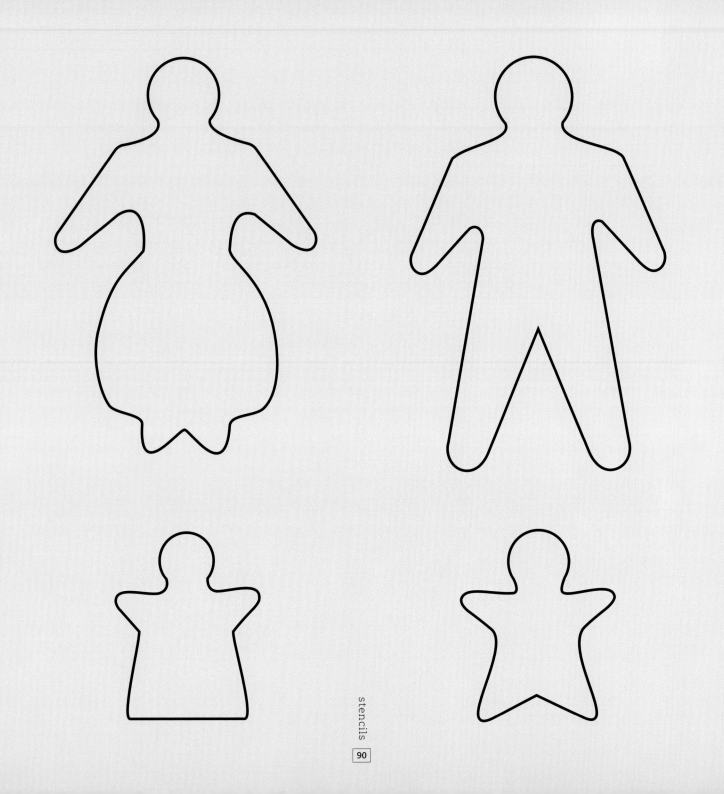

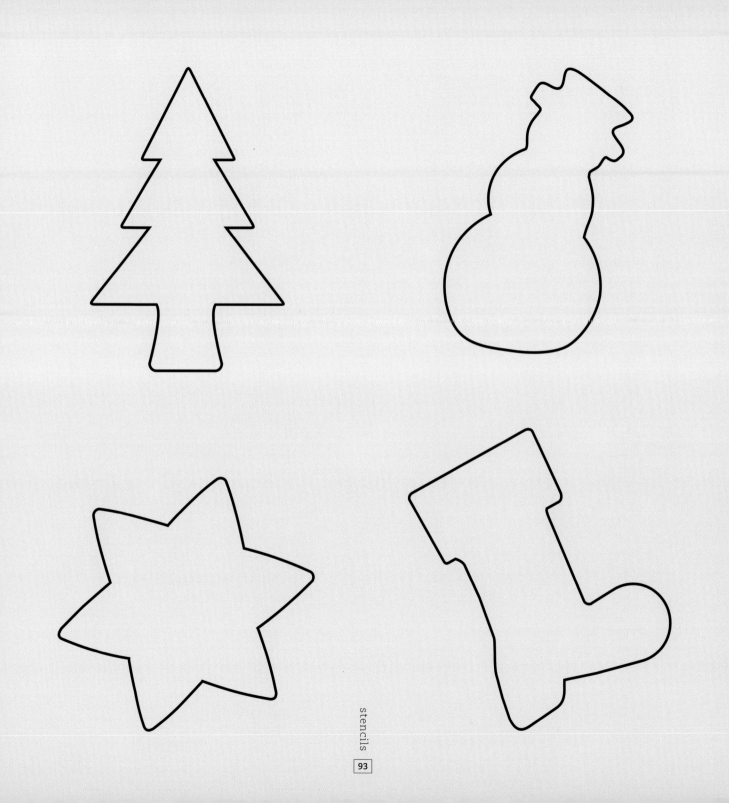

Index

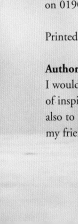

First published in 2005 by Conran Octopus Limited,
a part of Octopus Publishing Group,
2–4 Heron Quays, London E14 4JP
www.conran-octopus.co.uk

Publishing Director: Lorraine Dickey
Commissioning Editor: Katey Day
Editor: Sybella Marlow
Art Director: Jonathan Christie
Designer: Victoria Burley
Photography: Jean Cazals
Prop Stylist: Sue Rowlands
Home Economy: Bethany Heald
Production Manager: Angela Couchman

British Cataloguing-in-Publication Data.
A catalogue record for this book is available from the British Library.

ISBN 1 84091 444 0

To order please ring Conran Octopus Direct
on 01903 828503

Printed and bound in China

Author's Acknowledgments
I would like to thank my mum for always giving me such great ideas and bundles
of inspiration. Thanks to Kitchen Craft for use of their cookie cutters. A big thank you
also to Susie Plant and Bethan Woodyatt for all the testing and typing, not to mention
my friends and neighbours for the calories gained while helping me taste all the cookies.